# SEXISM IN INDIAN EDUCATION
## The Lies We Tell Our Children

# SEXISM IN INDIAN EDUCATION

## The Lies We Tell Our Children

### Narendra Nath Kalia

**VIKAS PUBLISHING HOUSE PVT LTD**
New Delhi Bombay Bangalore Calcutta Kanpur

VIKAS PUBLISHING HOUSE PVT LTD
5 Ansari Road, New Delhi 110002
Savoy Chambers, 5 Wallace Street, Bombay 400001
10 First Main Road, Gandhi Nagar, Bangalore 560009
8/1-B Chowringhee Lane, Calcutta 700016
80 Canning Road, Kanpur 208004

1V02K4001

ISBN 0 7069 0809 0

Printed at Dhawan Printing Works, 26-A Mayapuri, New Delhi 110064

*To my mother who seldom doubted my father,*
*and to my father who never allowed her to*

# Acknowledgements

I am indebted to Lou Kriesberg, Swami Agehananda Bharati and Raj Singh for patiently demonstrating the need to separate the significant from the trivial.

Jo Ann Wypijewski helped me through the final revision. Without her skills and conscientiousness, the book could not have been completed in time.

I am grateful to K.B. Vaid, Tracy Lynn, George Zito, Alok Mukherjee, for their editorial comments; to Linda Brasington, Beth Howe, Mergo Holland, Gary Spencer, Aman Patel, Chandra Kant, Mrs Yovan, Jugal Arora and Dilip Bhargava for their support, suggestions and enthusiasm.

Thanks is too trivial a word to express my appreciation to A., ANK, DNK and RNK who sustained me during the years I was working on this study.

# List of Tables

# Contents

# Contents

# CHAPTER I

# Why Study Sexism in Indian Textbooks?

. . .the fact that the so called psychological differences between the two sexes arise. . .out of social conditioning will have to be widely publicized and people made to realize that the stereotypes of "masculine" and "feminine" personalities do more harm than good.

—Education Commission of India, 1965.

God has made these women cent per cent stupid. I mean they have no brains at all.

—From the Hindi language instruction textbook, 1975, prescribed for the high schools of Rajasthan. Annual enroll-ment: 192,000 students.

## Indian Education and Sex Role
## Detraditionalization as Planned Change

Before 1974, Indian school curriculums generally followed the patriarchal tradition which type-cast individuals in unequal, gender-based roles. Boys were prepared to achieve in the market-place, while girls were trained to obey and please in the home.

At the inception of its educational policies for independent India, the Indian government proposed to develop a curriculum which promoted the sex role equality. Recognizing the "funda-mental and basic equality between men and women," it envision-ed an educational system that would provide the basis for a new society where "*the biological fact of sex will play a minor role*" and where an individual would not be forced "to conform to a

predetermined pattern of behavior on the basis of his/her sex"
(Education Commission, India, 1965:4, emphasis in the original).
Unlike traditional India, the social life of modern Indian
citizens was intended to develop as a joint venture for men and
women. Men would share the responsibilities of parenthood and
home-making; women would be free to engage in activities traditionally assigned to men. The textbooks were to help prepare
individuals for this era of equality between the sexes; to inspire
*"each sex to develop a proper respect towards the other"* (Ibid.,
p. 4, emphasis in the original).

As far back as 1965, Indian educational policy-makers talked
of intensive efforts to eradicate all traditional concepts of female
inferiority.

> . . .it is unscientific to divide tasks and subjects on the basis of
> sex and to regard some of them as 'masculine' and others as
> 'feminine'. Similarly, the fact that the so-called psychological
> differences between the two sexes arise, not out of sex but out
> of social conditioning, will have to be widely publicized and
> people will have to be made to realize that stereotypes of
> 'masculine' and 'feminine' personalities do more harm than
> good (Ibid., p. 5).

The fundamental duties proposed under the 44th Amendment
to the Indian Constitution reiterated a similar goal in calling upon Indian citizens to ". . .remove any practice derogatory to the
dignity of women" (*The Overseas Hindustan Times*, Sept. 16,
1976:1).

### State Control of Indian Textbooks

The preparation and approval of Indian school textbooks is
a highly centralized and mostly state-controlled enterprise.
Initially, the private publishers controlled the Indian textbook
market. Then, the Secondary Education Commission (1952-
1953) found serious flaws in the prescribed textbooks. As a
result, various state governments set up organizations to lower
the prices and upgrade the quality of textbooks by: 1) taking
over the production of textbooks and/or 2) improving the
machinery for approving textbooks submitted by private publishers. At the national level, the Central Bureau of School Text-

books and later the National Council of Educational Research and Training (NCERT), were entrusted with the task of developing guidelines for the states. Following the recommendation of the Education Commission (1964-1966:405), the National Board of School Textbooks was established in 1969 (Biswas and Aggarwal, 1972:91-95).

By the end of 1971, all states were reported to have set up appropriate agencies to produce school textbooks (NCERT, 1971). As a result, India's educational policy makers enjoy an almost dictatorial control over the content and format of Indian school textbooks.

## Modernization and Sex Role Detraditionalization

Modernization is an antecedent of sex role change.[1] In the course, of modernization, norms change causing individuals to redefine their social situation and transcend the boundaries of tradition. The pressures of urbanization tend to cut into gender differentiation (Holter, 1972:232). As women gain access to marketplace occupations, they increasingly realize how gender based stratification weakens the female by calculatedly excluding her from decision-making.

As an ideology, modernization also promotes the notion that similar options should be made available to all citizens, regardless of their sex, age, race and class. It is difficult to sustain ideologies fostering sex role inequality in supposedly democratic societies where modernization involves increased dissemination of information.

## Why this Study?

Given the above, one should be able to assert that the contents of the school textbooks in independent India do not typecast male and female characters in traditional, sexist models. However, there is no comprehensive analysis of sexism and/or sex role models in textbooks used by Indian adolescents. Our study attempts to fill this gap.

## Focus

Ours is a study of sexism and sex roles in Indian school textbooks. Sexism is an ideology which propagates inherent inequality between the sexes to support institutions that relegate women to traditional subservience.

The following four premises serve as our points of departure: 1. Education is an effective agent of socialization. 2. There is a positive correlation between sex role changes and the overall detraditionalization of developing societies. 3. The Indian government claims that it is committed to a policy of promoting sex role equality through Indian schools. 4. Since the production of textbooks in India is state-controlled and centralized, the educational policy-makers are empowered to ensure that the content of Indian textbooks complies with their declared goal of sex role equality.

In light of these premises, this study explores the differences between the traditional sex role model and the sex role model presented in the post-independence textbooks. To determine the differences between the two models, we formulated twelve hypotheses. These hypotheses are related to sex role imagery, male-centered language, anti-feminism, modes and models of achievement, gender-based dominance in decision-making, authority relationships, sex role victimization, sex-based division of labor, and occupational modeling.

In testing these hypotheses, we intended to compare the traditional sex role stereotypes, as depicted in the traditional sex role model constructed from pre-independence literary sources, with the sex role stereotypes in the post-independence school textbooks (hereinafter referred to as PITB). We hypothesized that:

H-1. As compared to the traditional literary stereotypes, the sex role imagery in the PITB will portray the members of both sexes as whole human beings and not merely in terms of their stereotypic masculine/feminine attributes.

H-2. The number of male authors in the PITB will not be far higher than that of female authors.

H-3. As compared to the sexism of the traditional linguistic usage, the PITB will not use nouns or pronouns that exclude females in generalizations about human society or the world.

H-4. As compared to the predominantly negative role-image of the female in traditional literary sex role stereotypes, the PITB will not foster contempt for women by including anti-feminine statements that put down women in general.

H-5. Among the subjects of biography, the PITB will not

depict males as representing an extremely high proportion of significant achievers.

H-6. Among the subjects of biography in the PITB, the parental and marital roles of a female shall not be highlighted as more essential to her identity than to the identity of a male.

H-7. Unlike the traditional sex role-based segregation of a "man's" and a "woman's" work, the PITB will depict both the male and female subjects of biography as performing marketplace as well as non-marketplace domestic activities.

H-8. The males will not constitute a heavy majority of leading characters in the PITB.

H-9. In decision-making situations involving the sexes, the PITB will not depict the male as more likely to dominate the decision-making process, nor will his right to dominate be derived from his sex role prerogatives rather than from his problem-solving abilities or other competency.

H-10. The PITB will not depict the male as more likely to be dominant-cooperative in social and marketplace authority relationships, while depicting the female as more likely to be cooperative-subservient.

H-11. The females in the PITB will not be victimized to a greater extent than the males through evaluative degradation, role restraint and actual physical violation.

H-12. As compared to the traditionally sexist division of labor, the range and diversity of occupations in the PITB will be similar for males and females.

*Plan of Chapters*

In Chapter 2, we outline our methodology, describe our sample and discuss the limitations of this study. In Chapter 3, drawing from the research on pre-independence literary sources, we construct a heuristic model of traditional sex role stereotypes. In Chapters 4, 5, 6, 7 and 8, we test hypotheses 1 through 12 against the results of our content analysis of the PITB. In Chapter 9, we compare the PITB sex role model with the traditional sex role model. Chapter 10 includes a summary of our conclusions and suggestions for desexistizing textbooks.

## FOOTNOTES

[1]There is little consensus among social theorists on the attributes of modernization (Schnailberg, 1970). For definitional purposes we will use the before/after model to distinguish between traditional and modern societies. We include the predominance of universal achievement norms and a high degree of social—not necessarily vertical—mobility as attributes of modernization. A society ceases to be traditional in the process of becoming more urban than rural, more literate than illiterate more industrialized than not.

We concede that such ideal types are only inadequate substitutes for scientifically validated generalizations, but any change minimally involves two terminal stages of structural transformation. We may not always be able to predict exactly *how* the transformed society would look. But if we do not make a few assumptions about the differences between the earlier and the later social structures, we would not know what changes to look for. We have assumed that societies can be classified by the degree to which they exhibit one set of attributes over the other, and we dichotomize the non-modern from the modern on the basis of contrasting adjectives.

Conklin's (1973) data on emerging conjugal role patterns in joint families of India show how education may help spread the ideology of equal roles between husband and wife even before the arrival of significant industrialization. For a dissenting note, see Kapadia's (1966:369) interpretation of B. Kuppuswamy's (1957) survey where he hints that education and economic considerations do not outweigh the impact of ideology. Obviously, these earlier studies do not differentiate between ideology as the product of childhood socialization, and ideology as a set of consciously acquired preferential schema during adulthood.

CHAPTER II

# Sample and Methodology

### Sample Textbooks

Our sample included 20 Hindi and 21 English language text-books used for classroom instruction in high school, higher secondary, and pre-university curriculums (Classes IX to XI) in the following five areas of India: Haryana, Punjab, Rajasthan, Uttar Pradesh (all states) and Delhi (a Union territory). Also included were the textbooks prepared by the National Council of Educational Research & Training (NCERT). The NCERT texts are used by the Central Board of Secondary Education and states other than those included in our sample.[1] All the 41 textbooks, listed in Appendix H, were either prepared or approved by state agencies.[2] As of 1976 the annual readership for these textbooks was more than thirteen lakh (1.3 million) students.[3]

Other states of India could have been included in the sample, but we restricted the sample to five states for the following reasons: 1) As compared to the rest of the country, these states roughly represent the core of what is generally referred to as Northern India, a geographical terrain with broadly similar cultural patterns. 2) We wanted to include the texts form a language other than English. All the states in our sample (with the exception of Punjab) use Hindi *and* English as their languages of instruction. Including other states would have involved examining the textbooks in more than one regional language. 3) Many of the books included in our sample. particularly the texts prepared by NCERT and books used by the Central Secondary Board of Education System, are used throughout the country.

### Lessons

The textbooks contained a total of 740 lessons. We did not

content analyze any poems. The ambiguity of their meaning and the elasticity of their structures restricted their amenability to content analysis. We further excluded those lessons which did not contain the following: 1) human characters, 2) significant roles assigned to human actors, or 3) social situations involving human actors.[4]

We selected 353 lessons for content analysis.[5] These lessons were divided into five categories: story, play, biography, essay, and other (memoirs, commentaries). More than half the lessons were classified as stories (58%). The remaining 42% were thus divided: biographies (20%, N=71), plays (10%, N=35), essays (5%, N=17) and other (7%, N=25).

While reading the lessons, we also tried to determine the probable origins of their plots. The plots were divided into three categories of origin—Indian, non-Indian, and indeterminable. We could not determine the origins of the plots for only two lessons (0.6%). Of the remaining 351 lessons, 56% (N=197) belonged in the category of plots with Indian origins, while 44% (N=154) had plots of Indian origin. In the lessons with plots of Indian origin, we coded the source of plots in one of the following categories: 1) religious mythology, 2) history, 3) folk literature or 4) fiction. The majority (55%, N=195) of the Indian origin lessons had plots from either fictional or historical sources.[6]

## METHODOLOGY

### Content Analysis

We have used content analyis as our method of analysis. To gather evidence for testing our hypotheses, we made inferences by systematically identifying specified characteristics within texts (Stone *et al*, 1965: 5). While using content analysis, social scientists have generally viewed frequency as a good index of the intensity and importance of an item in a text (Pool, 1959:194; Baldwin, 1942: 168). We tried to delineate the PITB sex role model by indexing the frequency and distribution of characteristics, activities, occupations, sex role, behavior expectancy, authority relationships, etc., in the PITB.

In its earlier days, content analysis was heavily quantitative. In its latter-day usage, however, the quantitative and qualitative techniques have been combined (Carney, 1972:53). In our analysis we have treated the two approaches as complementary.[7]

This study involves a comparison of two models to verify a theoretical perspective. We have used non-content analysis data to verify the results of content analysis findings. The data gathered by frequency counts have been processed through SPSS (Statistical Package for Social Scientists) and Fortran IV Alpha programs. The data not amenable to statistical analysis have been presented in the form of non-quantitative observations. Both kinds of data were used to test the hypotheses stated earlier.

The systems of reference have been used to denote the source of a citation. Numerals preceded by L identify the source as the lesson number, e.g., L-002, L-239. A textbook is identified in the following manner: In 38: 135, for example, the first two digits (38) represent the textbook ID number; the next three digits (135) denote the page number in the textbook. The lessons are listed in Appendix A. The textbooks are listed in Appendix H.

### Inter-Coder Reliability

The coding of non-quantitative data for content analysis is vulnerable to the coders' bias. While reading a lesson, two coders may interpret it differently. To avoid this, our coders' tasks were simplified to well-defined frequency counting with clear instructions for gathering evidence according to the format provided by the instruments of analysis (Appendix I). The coders were asked to refrain from creative interpretation. All English and Hindi lessons were read twice. The occupations and image lists, prepared during the first reading, were verified during the second reading.

Less than 10% of entries in the two lists needed to be changed during the second reading. Most alterations involved erroneous repetitions, or a non-existent image-occupation originally entered by mistake. Although this attrition rate of approximately 10% was similar for the Hindi and English language lists, only the English language lessons were read by two different coders. In the English language lessons, therefore, our inter-coder reliability reached a satisfactory level of 90% congruence.

### Limitations of the Sample

Three limitations of our sample need to be stated:

    1) Our sample contained only English and Hindi language

instruction textbooks from four north Indian states and a Union
territory. The need to limit the textbooks to a manageable number prompted this restriction. We did not reject the possibility
that sex role models in regional Indian languages may vary from
the models projected in Hindi and English literature; however,
given the dominance of patriarchal ideology, we presumed that
such deviation would be insignificant.

2) We were mainly looking at the message, the manifest
content related to the depiction of sex role stereotypes in the textbooks. As is sometimes done in propaganda analysis, we have not
empirically and separately investigated the intent of authors, nor
experimentally identified the specific effects of messages on a
particular audience.

3) We would have liked to content analyze some pre-
independence textbooks to generate the base for our traditional
model, but a satisfactory number of pre-independence textbooks
for the grades, geographical area, and languages comparable to
our PITB model were not available. We were restricted to compare the PITB model with a traditional model, based on secondary research of the general pre-independence Indian literature.
This, however, need not affect the validity of our comparison.
Neither did the use of secondary data affect the issue of equivalence. Our review of some pre-independence textbooks revealed
that, as in the PITB, most of their materials and themes were
directly borrowed from the inventory of themes and treatments
provided by the classic Indian literary tradition. Overall, it would
be safe to assume that the characters, plots, themes, and ideological preference of what the anthropologists call the "great
tradition" in Indian literature determined the content of pre-
independence textbooks.

The findings on the sex role stereotypes and the models of life
portrayed in the pre-independence literature serve as an ade-
quate source for constructing a heuristic model for comparative
purposes. We have constructed this model in the next chapter.

FOOTNOTES

[1]Of the total in the sample, half the textbooks were prescribed for
higher secondary, 39% were used for high school, and 12% were pres-

cribed for preparatory or pre-university curricula. The 41 textbooks in our sample were prescribed by a total of seven agencies: 1) Five school boards of Delhi, Haryana, Punjab, Rajasthan, Uttar Pradesh; 2) Central Board of Secondary Education and 3) NCERT. Rajasthan represented the largest number, 11 (27%), in the sample. The number of textbooks and percentages for the other prescribing agencies are as follows: Uttar Pradesh, 8 (19%); Central Board of Secondary Education, 6 (15%); NCERT, 6 (15%); Kurukshetre, 5 (13%) Punjab, 3 (7%) and Haryana, 2 (5%). Haryana and Punjab score low because some of the texts used in these regions were content analyzed under the original category of texts produced by NCERT. Both Haryana and Punjab, for example, use English Reader Book IV. The lessons in these readers are taken from the material used in compilations prepared by NCERT and the Central Institute of English, Hyderabad. Since we had content analyzed the material included in the English Reader Book IV of Haryana and Punjab as part of the NCERT texts and text for other states, Book IV was not content analyzed again.

To collect our sample of textbooks, we travelled to Lucknow, Chandigarh, Jaipur and Delhi during May and June of 1975. We tried to include most of the Hindi and English language instruction textbooks for the areas and agencies specified above. Our task was made easier by the fact that almost all Indian schools (with the exception of some "public schools" that follow the Senior Cambridge Syllabus) use only such textbooks as have already been approved by a state agency. It is possible, despite disclaimers by booksellers in various cities and the storekeepers at NCERT, that we might have missed a few books which were either prescribed later that year, or were not in print at the time of our visit. To double-check, we examined the 1974 and 1975 lists of Hindi and English language instruction textbooks prescribed for our geographical regions, Central Board of Secondary Education, and NCERT.

[2]Given the hierarchical and bureaucratic nature of educative procedures in India, it is clear that in the eighties, school textbook production will be totally centralized, giving the state an overwhelming control over the ideological content of textbooks.

[3]In terms of the sex ratio of the total student population in our sample regions, Delhi had the most equivalent sex ratio—59% male, 41% female. Uttar Pradesh displayed the most inequivalent sex ratio—86% male vs. 14% female. Rajasthan, with 85% male and Haryana, with 81% male, were closer to the inequivalent sex ratio in their student populations. Punjab with 67% male and 33% female was in the middle and closer to Delhi.

We could not find any exact figures of student enrollment for the Central Board of Secondary Education. Since the Indian government statistics which we used did not categorize pre-university students separately, we deemed it safe to presume that the "Class IX and Above" category included pre-university level students.

For the academic year ending 1969, the *total* student enrollment in *all* the Indian states and Union territories for 'Class IX and Above' was reported to be more than six million. For the geographic area covered in our sample, a total student population for the same period and class levels was reported as more than one and a quarter million (N= 1,348,234). While the national male and female student ratio was 75% male to 25% female. The sex ratio for our sample was 80% male to 20% female (Table 1).

TABLE 1

*Students in Schools, by Sex, Class IX and Above Sex of Student*

| Prescribing Agency/Region | Boys % | Girls % | Total 100 % |
|---|---|---|---|
| Delhi | 78,147 (59%) | 53,271 (41%) | 131,418 |
| Haryana | 95,059 (81%) | 22,404 (19%) | 117,463 |
| Punjab | 119,383 (67%) | 58,174 (33%) | 177,557 |
| Rajasthan | 163,336 (85%) | 28,703 (15%) | 192,039 |
| Uttar Pradesh | 625,732 (86%) | 104,025 (14%) | 729.757 |
| Central Board | Treated as subsumed under the data for regional student populations. | | |
| *Total* | *1,081,657 (80%)* | *266,577 (20%)* | *1,348,234 (100%)* |

*Source:* Ministry of Education & Social Welfare, Government of India 1974. Education in India, 1968-69. New Delhi: Controller of Publications pp. 185-86.

In response to my phone inquiry, the director of the Central Board of Secondary Education, Dr. G.L. Bakshi, supplied the figure of 18,931 as the total number of students appearing for examination under the Central Board in 1977. Since the Ministry of Education statistics for the total population of students do not categorize the Central Board students separately, we have presumed the number of students enroled in the Central Board system to be included in the total enrollment figures.

[4]The only exception was Lesson 17, in which the plot contained two animals behaving quite like humans while acting out their sex roles.

[5]Sixty-five per cent (N=230) of these lessons were written in English and 35% (N=123) in Hindi. Two novels, Text ID # 22 and Text ID # 37 were each treated as a single lesson. Plots that continued over more than one lesson were treated as a single lesson.

[6]It was impossible to pinpoint the original year of publication for all the literary materials used as lessons in our sample. We did not divide our sample into two sets of lessons actually written before and after 1947, the year of Indian independence. A random check, however,

established that the year of original publication is not very helpful in determining the nature of its sex role contents. Some lessons that could have been written after 1947 contain themes supporting the unequal sex role relationships, Other lessons that may have been written prior to 1947 contain elements conducive to sex role equality. Anti-feminine statements, for example, occur in all kinds of lessons written before and after 1947.

The lessons in our sample include some famous Western works from Shakespeare, Jules Verne, Hans Christian Anderson and others. Some of the plots have been rewritten to suit the comprehension levels of Indian youngsters. We examined these plots to see if they have been "Indianized" to the extreme. Most of the rewriting is faithful to the original. We did not detect any transformation in the retold plots to warrant an examination of the process of rewriting as a unit of analysis by itself.

[7]We also believe that a content analysis need not be limited solely to manifest content (those items that are clearly stated in the text). To bring out the latent and manifest meanings, the focus of a content analysis should be extended to include the latent content (items derived from an interpretative reading of the meaning between the lines) as well (Holsti, 1969: 12 ff.).

# CHAPTER III

# Traditional Sex Role Model

In selecting literature as our basic source for sex role themes, we have assumed that the literature of a society is a reliable indicator of its sociological realities as well as its ideals. To outline the traditional sex role model, we have used two kinds of secondary material: 1) Research studies that utilize literary sources to depict *social conditions* in India during various periods. 2) Research studies that use literary sources to delineate *sex role models* in Indian society in different historical periods. In this chapter, we will present three kinds of evidence from the pre-independence literature: 1. Themes relating to *sex role behavior in general*, 2. Themes that are conducive to *sex role inequality*, and 3. Themes that are conducive to *sex role equality*.

## TRADITIONAL SEX ROLES: THE IDEAL MALE, FEMALE AND THEIR EDUCATION

### The Ideal Male

As personified in Ram—the *maryaada-purushottam*—an ideal male was trained in law, warfare, logic, diplomacy, and recreative arts. He was respectful to elders and betters, fair to his equals, and kind to those below him. He was handsome, sturdy, perceptive, compassionate, just, adorable, kind, well-mannered, mild yet firm and never, never self-indulgent (Vyas, 1967: 166-67).

The Hindu ideal emphasized the overall grooming and prenuptial chastity of the groom. Although during conditions of adversity, a husband could desert his wife, as *pati* and *bhartaar* he was expected to provide for the females of his households. He was also obliged to sleep with his wife during the *ritukaala*—the post-menstrual period when her sexual desire peaked. He was

responsible for ensuring her participation in all religious ceremonies. He was expected to be kind and impartial to all his
wives. In order to fulfil his role properly, a husband was
expected to *protect* and *control* his wife.

## The Ideal Female

In the Vedic tradition, the female was perceived as God's gift
to man. The Vedas spoke of her as a joy-giver, a caretaker, a
fellow sufferer and above all, an equal partner—*sahdharmini*.
The female of the Vedic era was not totally confined to her
home, but household chores were her major responsibility
(Upadhyaya, 1974: 45). This emphasis on domestic work continued in the lifestyle of the Epic's maiden. The lower-class girls
even helped their parents in their occupational work (Jayal,
1966: 20).

In Mughal India, while the lives of commoner housewives
revolved around everyday domestic chores, the indoor activities
of the upper-class women in harems including smoking, drinking,
playing chess, dancing and singing. The outdoor activities of the
royal females involved occasional trips to fairs, festivals, pilgri-
mages and, at times, civil or military expeditions in the company
of men (Misra, 1967: Ch. 5, 6 and 8). The upper-class female's
participation in mixed outdoor activities steadily declined during
the Mughal period. Only the lower-class female, as a result of
her economic position, continued to be less restricted by the
constraints of purdah.

## Property Rights of the Female

Though the evidence is inconclusive, it is possible that the
Vedic daughters had an assigned share in their father's property
(Upadhyaya, 1973: 213). Nevertheless, property rights of the
female were governed for the most part by a double standard
similar to that which governed her freedom. In principle, she
always had some kind of property rights. The *kanyaa-dhan* (the
bridal gifts given by parents to their daughter at the time of her
marriage) and occasional gifts from the husband became the
wife's property. She was supposedly free to use and dispose of
such articles at her own discretion. In practice, however, a
woman seldom disputed the supremacy of menfolk with regard
to the household property.

*Education and Training of the Males and Females*

Under the gurukul system of ancient India, the actual instruction was conducted in the home of preceptor. Where the pupil was expected to live.[1] This system was naturally more favorable to males. For practical training in agriculture, husbandry, trade, masonry, etc., the students were mostly apprenticed under a master.

The curriculum of education for females in the Vedic period included mythology, literature, music, elementary rules of prosody, fine arts and sometimes even the use of the bow and arrow (Upadhyaya, 1974: Ch. 7). The heroines of the epics emerge as literat and articulate individuals (Jayal, 1966: 21-29). A host of female scholars are reported during the 600 to 1000 A.D. era (Sharma, 1966). There are numerous descriptions of *paravraajikaas*—the female hermits who narrated sacred tales and imparted religious instruction. Although uncommon, military education for women was not unheard of (Vyas, 1967: 102).

Pursuant to the growth of towns, *madarsaahs* were also opened in the neighborhoods of medieval Indian towns. Whether this contributed to a rise in female enrollment is not clear. During the Mughal era and up until the nineteenth century, only princesses and upper middle class girls were instructed by private tutors in philosophy, grammar, mathematics, rhetoric, music, and religious literature. Girls so educated were reported to have participated in public literary discussions, though more for fun than as the crowning of a successful higher education (Mukerji, 1972: Ch. 3). Among the commoners, very few girls were allowed to continue their formal education after finishing the primary school. Thus, the majority of both Hindu and Muslim girls remained illiterate, learning no more than needlework, cooking, embroidery and other household skills from their female elders (Misra, 1967: 138). Given the prevalent sex role models, training in household work was considered both proper and sufficient for the female.

*Females in Marketplace Occupations*

Despite the strong non-occupational slant of female education, some women were employed in various marketplace occupations. From the Vedic period onward, the courtesans formed a part of the socio-political backdrop (Sharma, 1966: 27). Almost every court in India had its share of female prostitutes (*ganikaas*), singers, dancers, messengers, and *nagarvadhus*. In the time of Harsha, women worked as personal attendants, doorkeepers, ushers, beetle carriers, flower-bearers, kitchen supervisors, wine cellar keepers, and armed guards. In Mughal India, women were reported to have acted as soothsayers and spies (Misra, 1967: 82-83). Other marketplace activities of the females, in leadership roles, are discussed later in this chapter.

## THEMES CONDUCIVE TO SEX ROLE INEQUALITY

### Devaluation of the Female Principle

Exactly what factors caused the fall of the Great Mother as a manifestation of the female principle are not clear. The males in early eras, ignorant of their role in the mysteries of reproduction, could have resented the females' mystical status as child-bearer and set out to take their revenge by degrading the female principle (de Reincourt, 1974: 165). The patriarchal *weltanschauung* of early farming societies systematically degraded the female principle. The universal promotion of the sun as a dominant mythological symbol marked the transformation whereby most female myths were reinterpreted solely to promote the supremacy of the male principle.[2] A similar process of psychological mutation, particularly downgrading the powers of the Godmother, could be detected in Indian literature, beginning with the Vedas.

### Anti-Feminine Statements

The denunciation of females as a group began with aspersions cast in the Vedic literature: ". . .the mind of woman brooks not discipline. Her intellect hath little weight. . .with woman, there can be no lasting friendship. . ." (Upadhayaya, 1974: 159). Though Buddha reluctantly allowed women to become Sisters, establish convents and join the order, he considered them inferior to the males. In his death bed conversation with his favorite pupil Ananda, Buddha outlined a principle for behavior toward women, instructing that Buddhist monks should avoid them because, "Women are soon angered, Ananda; women are full of passion. . .envious. . .stupid. . .women have no place in public assemblies. . ." (Coomarswamy, 1928: 164). Mahabharata enjoined women to refrain from studying Vedas. The Epics went

to absurd lengths to portray women as carnally insatiable lewds.
"They are inconsistent, irreligious, licentious, fickle, crooked,
ominous catalysts of conflict leading to the destruction of
families, cities, and nations" (Jayal, 1966: 228-230).

The vituperations of Manu set the tone for the denunciation
of women in Indian literature. After a token tribute to the need
for honoring them, Manu portrayed women as base and ignoble
subjects. No woman, Manu recommended, should attempt to be
independent, even in her own house. In childhood, she should
obey her father, in youth her husband. If her husband dies
before her, she should defer to her sons. Single, married or
widowed, at no point in her life should she make her own
decisions (Buehler, 1964: 147-151).

Literature between 600 and 1000 A.D. continued to reflect the
tone of Manu in its anti-feminine stance. Even the poets of
*bhakti-kaal*, an otherwise enlightened group of folk writers, denounced the female as the gate to hell, more poisonous than
vipers and worthy of severe disciplining.

*Asceticism* (Women as the Source of Evil)

Asceticism, particularly the doctrine of *brahmcharya*, placed
an unusual emphasis upon the desirability of freedom from
sexual desires. The female, as a source of pleasure, was depicted
as a temptress. According to this image, women lacked the
moral strength of men. The scriptures are full of anecdotes in
which deceptive women act as decoys to distract the ascetics
from their higher spiritual pursuits.[3]

*Women as Commodity*

There is ample evidence to suggest that women were considered chattel. Kings, even commoners, bought and sold women as
slaves. In *ashvamedha* rites, kings offered their queens as part of
the fee to priests who could exchange them for money. A wife
was often considered expendable. After Laxman was seriously
wounded on the battlefield of Lanka, Ram exclaimed that a wife
could be found anywhere by anybody; but no so a brother
(Vyas, 1967: 125).

*Non-Preference for Daughters*

The birth of a girl was dreaded as early as the times of
Atharva Veda (Upadhayaya, 1974: 42). This notion seems to

have been canonized in corresponding social customs by the time of the Mughals. In most cases, the newly born female child was met with either unmixed disapproval, or with cold-blooded murder (Mukerjee, 1972: 1-27). Female infanticide has almost disappeared in independent India, but given the perpetuation of the dowry system, compounded by other problems which arranged marriages present for the bride's parents, the fear and disapproval of daughters has persisted to the present day.

## Preference for Sons

Conversely, the son and father have always had a special bond. The important information on kinship feuds, alliances, status mechanisms and occupational expertise was transmitted to the sons, not to the transient daughters. A son ensured generational continuity. Hindu mothers and fathers invariably preferred a son because a male heir was deemed a religious and economic necessity. The Indian inheritance laws continued to favor the male until 1950.

## Constraints on the Freedom of Choice for a Spouse

Though sometimes free to choose her spouse, the Indian girl was never totally free from parental and other kinship constraints. In Rigvedic India, marriages were cancelled when parents objected (Upadhyaya, 1974: 58). It was the duty of the father and brothers to assist the maiden in obtaining a worthy husband. If she erred in their opinion, they were entitled to intervene and decide what was best for her.

## Training for Subservience, Early Socialization of the Female as Pativrata

Once married, a woman was obliged to behave along strictly disciplined lines. Since the total self-denial required of a *pativrata* wife was not easy to achieve, the girl was trained for self-abnegation from early childhood. The Epics repeatedly detail the components of ideal womanhood, always insinuating that frail and fickle as women are, they need to be constantly reminded of their duties (Jayal, 1966: 103). From her infancy, the famale was indoctrinated with notions of duty, etiquette and moral obligation to make her a submissive daughter and an obedient wife.[4]

While a man's eligibility in marriage was judged by his intellectual, spiritual and wordly accomplishments, the female was expected to be pretty, soft-spoken, virtuous, self-controlled, genial, hospitable, chaste, pure, noble, humble, and dedicated to please her husband (Sharma, 1966:26). A husband was to be obeyed even when he was licentious, polygamous, cruel, and unreasonable.

As a *pativrata*, a woman was more of a devotee than a friend. As *proshita-patikaa*, she decorated herself for her husband's pleasure. Conversely, she did not use any cosmetics while her husband was away. As *janani*, she bore progeny for her husband. So important was the child-bearing function that a woman could gladly leave this world after she had borne sufficient number of children, preferably sons, to ensure the continuity of her husband's *vansh* (Jayal, 1966:119).

## Widowhood, Sutti and Jauhar

If she managed to outlive her husband, the Indian woman's lot was a sorry one. A general disapproval of widow remarriage, cofirmed by *Manusanhitaa*, came about in post-Vedic India, roughly 1000 B.C. The widow of the Epic period was expected to voluntarily plunge into the funeral pyre of her deceased husband. It was her ultimate gesture of affection and loyalty to him. Except in the lower classes where widow remarriage was permitted and encouraged, social pressures generally forced the majority of widows to commit sutti in the name of honor. Those who lived led a miserable life, burdened with guilt and restricted by taboos (Mukherjee, 1972:Ch. 4).

## The Double Standard

As in other traditional societies, the Indian tradition legitimized sex role inequality by applying different standards to male-female sexual conduct. According to Vatsyayan's *Kama Sutra*, the male (Nagrika) was free to have orgies at home to entertain his mistresses and friends. The wife, however, was not expected to enter the quarters reserved for the male's amorous adventures. With her husband's permission she might visit her relatives, a temple or a religious festival Otherwise, she had to confine herself strictly to demestic chores. Severe punishments were prescribed for any sexual indiscretion by the famale (Raghuvanshi, 1969:106-107).

*The "Stupid" Famle: A self-Fulfilling Prophecy*

It is little wonder that socialization into such role ideals produced women fit these roles. In a way, the "stupid female" represented the actualization of a self-fulfilling prophecy. Poisoned with a negative self-concept, handicapped by poor education, weakened by premature motherhood and condemned to domestic drudgery, the average traditional housewife might very well have been unfit for the company of the lively, educated, vivacious males. This, in trun, may have been responsible for socially legitimized and glamorous status enjoyed by courtesans, prostitutes and dancing girls in traditional India.

## THEMES CONDUCIVE TO SEX ROLE EQUALITY

*Male-Female Complementarity in the Indian Myth of Creation*

In contrast to the Chirstian stereotype of Eve, who is condemned for her role in events leading to the original sin, the pertinent mythological origin of sexual differentiation in Indian tradition occurs when the Universal Self, initially existent in the form of a man, lacked delight and desired a second for fulfillment. It divided itself in two parts. The male conjoined with the female and from this union arose the human race (Campbell, 1964:9-10). Though this event clearly affirmed the predominance of the masculine principle in a basically androgynous Universal Self, it did not hold woman responsible for any ethical tension. The female was created to complement the male, not to doom him.

The Sankhya school of philosophy further enhanced this complementarity by recognizing the necessity of a union between *purusa*, the male spirit, and *prakriti*, the female personification of matter, as a prelude to any creative action. In *Ardhanaarishwar*, the androgynous form of god Siva, the male and female were the complementary halves of a single entity.[5] As in *Ying-Yong*, this dichotomy indicated cooperation rather than any fundamental antagonism between the sexes.

*The Godmother Principle*

In the mythical support for the Great Godmother image, the earth and woman were unified as essential components of the life-giving female principle. In almost all civilizations—from the Minoan Crete to the Shang of China to the Indus Valley civilization—the woman was the earth itself and all that emanated from her womb was semantically denoted in the feminine gender. Unlike Western religious mythology in which the male principle dominates, the Great Mother in India has preserved her status in the Great Tradition as *Bhuvaneshwari* (Kali, *Grhadevi*) ruler of the World and devourer of evil. The Little Tradition also continues to exalt her as *Graam-Maataa*, the protectoress of the villages.

If the imagery used in describing the Vedic goddesses is any indicator of contemporary female stereotypes, the Vedic literature provides us with a set of powerful feminine role models. Lovely Usa, in her colorful forms, moves with the grace of an accomplished dancer. Aditi personifies freedom, while Saraswati is the patroness of learning and fine arts. As the embodiment of eternal cosmic energy, Vak aids the Creator in administering the universe, not as an assistant, but as an omniscient counterpart (Upadhyaya, 1974:211-212).

## Feminists in Traditional India

Another important reinforcement of the themes and images conducive to sex role equality came from thinkers who either criticized the deprecatory stereotyping of the female or assigned her a positive role in their thought systems. Varahmihir, the great astronomer, openly criticized treatment of women by his contemporaries. The poet Ban Bhatt opposed sutti (Thomas, 1966:281). Basava, a twelfth century South Indian Brahmin who founded the Lingayat sect, did not accept the doctrine of inherent male superiority. He endorsed widow remarriage, conditional divorce, and the consent of bridegroom in arranged marriages (Altekar, 1938).

*Mahanirvaana Tantra* approved of widow remarriage and conditional divorce if a girl became a widow before her marriage was consummated. Also, a woman married to an impotent man had the right to divorce him and remarry. The Tantrics condemned sutti and rape. An embodiment of the supreme *Shakti* pervading the universe, a female in the Tantric model could receive the mantra initiate another as a Guru. The Tantric doctrine suggested that whereas the male principle was inert in the universe, the female principle inspired all active virtues. For everyday life, *Mahanirvaana Tantra* thus enumerated the duties of a householder:

The householder should never punish his wife ... Whilst his own wife is living, (he) should never with wicked intent, touch another woman; otherwise, he is sure to go to hell. . . . The husband should never do anything that is unpleasant to her (Quoted in Thomas, 1966:277-78).

## Reverence for Motherhood

In the Rgvedic literature, the mother appears as a dominant actor in the household, people's assemblies and battlefields (Upadhyaya, 1974:4). In the Epics, she is higher than the preceptor and father. She raises heroes and diffuses intergenerational quarrels to keep families together (Jayal, 1966:Ch. 6). India's reverence for women as mothers is best stated by Shridharani (1941:109):

In the beginning, according to Indian mythology, was Shakti . . . .energy . . . a feminine gender. The cosmos was her creation, her child . . . It is the mother, not the father, who comes to mind first whenever the word 'creation' is mentioned. Woman's eternal energy, her natural ability to give and to feed life, to add cell to cell, make man look relatively unimportant to the scheme of things. . . All other loves, the loves of the betrothed, of married couples, of friends, of fathers for their sons, of brothers and sisters, are based on reciprocity . . . mother love alone can be one-sided. . . God is love, He should be concieved of as Mother and not Father.

## Lack of any Stigma Associated with a Daughter's Birth

Though the preference for a son is clear in the Vedas, the Upanishads prescribe a set of rituals for those who want a learned daugther to be born in their household (Upadhyaya, 1974:42). In the Epics. the birth of a daughter was not bemoaned, and Daughter-adoption was common. Sita, Kunti, and Shakuntala were all adopted daugthers. As *putridharmini*, the brotherless daughter could perform the funeral rites for her father and inherit property (Jayal, 1966).

## Freedom of Movement and Choice of Partners

The Rgvedic maiden was not a meek or shy creature like her later counterparts. Bold, strong and uninhibited, she was free to move in and outside her home. Maidens reportedly flocked in great numbers to *samans*—sports event that also served as arenas for mate-selection. Free to choose their husbands, the females did not hesitate in arguing out the choice of their partner with their elders. There was sufficient premarital sexual activity to indicate that the Vedic society provided legitimized, open access to single members of the opposite sex (Upadhyaya, 1974: Ch. 2).

In the Epics, the girls went to gardens for sports, and to mixed parties that provided ample opportunities for courtship (Vyas, 1967:102). A similar freedom of movement was later observed by a Western traveller in the late eighteenth century:

> A Hindu woman can go anywhere alone, even in the most crowded places, and she need never fear the impertinent looks and jokes of idle loungers . . . A house inhabited solely by women is a sanctuary which the most shameless libertine would not dream of violating (Dubois, 1928:340).

## Freedom to Perform Religious Rites

In the Epics era, most religious ceremonies were performed by spouses together. But if the husband was absent for some reason, the wife could perform the rites alone. Kausalya alone performed the *svasti yagna* to ensure felicity for her son (Vyas, 1967:112).

## Role Model of the Female as an Equal Participant

The Rgvedic rituals treated marriage as a communion of equals in which the bridegroom asked the bride to become his partner. The woman was expected to be his comrade, his *sakhi*. The two entered marriage as participants with equal status. This equality extended beyond the private sector. Albeit marginally, ladies of the Turk, Afghan and Mughal nobility were influential in the affairs of state (Misra, 1967: Ch. 4). Some commoner females of the Mughal era were reported to have inherited, owned and sold property. Other latter-day accounts indicated that Indian women generally enjoyed an effective role in the choice of spouses for her childern and other household matters (Raghuvanshi, 1969:106).

## Female Achievers as Role Models

Looking at the historical record, one is immediately struck by the impressive number of Indian females who broke the social barriers to rise to prominence and power. That their contemporaries did not treat them as deviants but as achievers, again confirms the duality of thought governing women's status in the Indian tradition.

In folklore and fiction, female achievers emerge, not as freaks, but as healthy manifestations of feminine energy in the dyad of Creation. A singificant number of Rgvedic hymns were ascribed to females whose excellence in composition and poetry equalled that of the male *rsis*. Bhaskarachary wrote to Lilavati asking her to teach mathematics to his daughter. In the *shastraartha* between Shankar and Madan Mishra, the latter's wife presided over the debate (Misra, 1967:3).

Many of the early Indian tribes were named after women (e.g., Kadravey, descendent of Kadru; Vinateya of Vinata; Diatyas of Diti and Danavas of Danu.) Women fought regularly in the armies of the aboriginal Dasas (Upadhyaya, 1974:187-88). Yuwan Chwang cited two *stri-raajyas*, women's kingdoms, in his travelogue. Marco Polo mentioned Rudramba, the thirteenth century Kakteya queen who fought her way to the throne and reconstructed her kingdom (Sengupta, 1974:129).

In medieval India, Tara Bai Ahalya Bai Holkar, and Rani Durga Vati took active part in statecraft. Majumdar mentions women as historians, accountants, judges, bailiffs and guards in the Vijay Nagar empire (1953:376). The women who entered and succeeded in marketplace occupations in British India are too numerous to be cited individually.[6]

*Concluding Remarks*

The Indian tradition regarding females appears charged with radical ambivalence. Seldom have women been concurrently extolled for their virtues and condemned for their vices with such passion. So continuous is the undercurrent of singificant themes conducive *both* to equalitarianism and inequalitarianism that almost all periods of Indian literature reflect this dichotomy. To avoid reductionism, we have treated themes conducive both to equality and inequality as relevant components of the traditional sex role model.

Despite the original dualism, there was a clear historical movement toward increasing sex role inquality in post-Vedic India. Sex role stratification during the era immediately preceding 1947 was generally more inequalitarian than equalitarian. As a result, these characteristics of the traditional sex role model also emerge in the pre-independence literary materials:

1. The proportion of male authors is far higher than that of female authors.

2. Males constitute a heavy majority of leading characters and subjects of biographic materials.

3. The language is overwhelmingly male centered.

4. The females are victimized to a greater extent than the males. Victimization includes verbal and physical abuse through evaluative degradation and role restraints.

5. The male is more likely to dominate decision-making situations between the sexes. His right to dominate is generally derived from his sex role rather than from his problem-solving abilities or other functional competency.

6. Both in social and marketplace (formal, vocational, business) relationships, the male is more likely to be dominant while the female is more likely to be cooperative and subservient.

7. Females in politics do have authority at all levels, but the instances of females holding high positions in marketplace authrity structures are rare and exceptional.

8. The traditional male is more likely to be independent, self-less, task-oriented, assertive, innovative, dominant, clever, strong (physically and in character), brave and generous; while the traditional female is likely to be dependent, selfless, confused, non-assertive, imitative, incompetent, fragile (in character), weak, fearful and petty.

9. The male is more likely to be trained in a formal setting to acquire skills for a marketplace occupation.

10. The males represent an extremely high proportion of singificant actors and achievers in marketplace activities and occupations.

11. Man's and woman's work is clearly distinguished.

### FOOTNOTES

[1]This section on education and training is based on Rawat, 1970.

[2]"In the Paleolithic mythical consciousness, the sun was the great hunter. The divinity of the sun, lord of time and space, was essentially masculine: the phallic sunbeams striking down on Mother Earth; a maleness whose rays impregnate the earth and cause the seed to germinate. From Spain to China, the prehistoric sun stood for maleness, individual

self-consciousness, intellect, and the glaring light of knowledge, as against the moon, ruler of the tide, the womb." (de Reincourt, 1974:35).

[3]For a preposterous elaboration of this view, see Chand, 1972, who believes that most of the current ills in the Indian society can be attributed to the inability of the modern Indian male to follow a path of restraint and curb the female's inherent lust.

[4]The scriptural support for male dominance begins in the Vedic literature. The Rgvedic goddess was subjected to male dominance and was seldom evaluated independent of her male associates (Upadhyaya, 1974: 41).

Ross (1961:137), in her study of the urban middle class Hindu family, demonstrates how the dominance model of sex role interaction still continues to affect the warmth of husband-wife relationships in the non-uclear families. In an attempt to assess the ties of affection and sentiment in family relationships, Ross rank-ordered the emotional attitudes of family members towards each other. The following rank order emerged from her mixed sample of 157 subjects: mother-son, brother-sister, brother-brother, father-son, father-children, husband-wife, sister-sister. The sample was taken in urbanized, middle class Bangalore where one would expect to find a higher rating ascribed to husband-wife relationships. But her data show that the mother-son relationship is still much more often stressed as being one of love and affection than is any other.

[5]"Also, when there was neither the creation, nor the sun, the moon, the planets, and the earth, and when darkness was enveloped in darkness, then the Mother, the Formless One, Maha-Kali, the the Great Power, was one with Maha-Kala, the Absolute" (Campbell, 1964:165) To a *Sakta*, "... the male side of the god was believed to relegate all his more onerous and troublesome executive functions to his female counterpart. And hence it has come to pass that the female side of the personal god is often more honoured and propitiated than the male" (Monier-Williams, 1887:181).

[6]In British India, Pandita Rama Bai led the movement for social reform to facilitate female education and widow remarriage. There were many female achievers in pre-independence India: Nawab Sultan Begum of Bhopal; Anandi Bai Joshi, the westren educated Hindu woman to become a practising doctor; Toru Dutt and Sarojini Naidu, international acclaimed poets; Rama Bai Ranade, social worker; Kamla Devi Chattopadhyay, the first woman to contest election for legislative assembly; Durga Bai Deshmukh; K. Ganguli, the first woman to speak from the Congress platform; Raj Kumari Amrit Kuar, President of All-India Women's Conference; Rustomji Fardoonji, Hansa Mehta, Vijay Laxmi Pandit, Sushila, Nayyar, S. Muthulaxmi Reddy, Kasturba, Janaki Devi Bajaj, Mridula Sarabhai and Leelavati Munshi. These are just a few examples of women who entered marketplace occupations and the socio-political activities of pre-independence India. For a detailed discussion of female achievers in teaching, medicine, law, journalism, business, aviation, industry, films, fine arts, social work, literature, sports and public life during the twentieth century, see Asthana, 1974, Ch. 9.

CHAPTER IV

# Images Assigned to the Male and Female Characters

The wide body of beliefs, epigrams, treaties and jokes demonstrates how kings and comedians alike have long felt obliged to comment on the nature of the sexes. The variety of such lore is not as interesting as the amount of confidence it commands as a guide to actual sex role behavior.

In samples from a cross-section of populations, psychologists have found a substantial agreement on popularly held beliefs regarding the personality traits of men and women (Deaux, 1976:13). In the traditional stereotype, males are independent, competitive, task-oriented, clever, brave, strong in physique and character. The stereotypic female, on the other hand, is generally considered dependent, selfless, confused, non-aggressive, imitative, essentially a follower, incompetent, fragile, weak and fearful. The customary roles of femininity and masculinity destine the woman to be a housewife and mother, while the man invents, builds empires and rules the world by virtue of his "inherent superiority".

How does the sex role imagery in the PITB differ from these common stereotypes? To determine the extent to which the PITB model deviates from the traditional model, this chapter will test the following hypotheses:

H-1. As compared to the traditional literary stereotypes, the sex-role imagery in the PITB will portray the members of both sexes as whole human beings and not merely in terms of their traditional, stereotypic masculine feminine attributes.

## Methodology

For our analysis, we decided to use the term "image" rather than "characteristic," "adjective," or "personality trait". In our lessons, we found a large number of sex role traits that were attributed directly to characters. There were also instances where the plot etched a sex role stereotype by inference rather than definitive articulation. The word "image" was considered specific enough to include all the adjectives assigned to a character and comprehensive enough to accommodate other shares of meaning.

The scope of an image was expanded to include closely associated words and images (see Appendix B). The count for the image "compassionate," for example, also included the following adjectives: understanding, considerate, passionate, sensitive, civil, concerned, comforming, thoughtful and sweet. Such elaboration prevented duplication.

We compiled separate lists of favourable images ascribed to the two sexes. When an image referring to a particular sex occurred more than once in a single lesson, it was listed only once. The repetition of a particular image in the same lesson was cited as the evidence to support an image, but was not cited in the image count. The image count was used as an indicator of the salience of an image. The numerical salience of an image indicates the number of lessons in which the image appeared as an attribute of one or more characters. The numerals following a specific image, e.g. compassionate (34), represent its salience scope.

To determine the image count, every lesson was read and coded twice. I read and coded all Hindi and English language lessons in the first reading. The task of second reading of English lessons was distributed among six coders, all American, English-speaking students at Syracuse University. Since no coder with proficiency in Hindi was available, I myself performed the second reading for Hindi lessons.

To organize the evidence for images, we used four broad categories: 1) intellect, 2) character, 3) feelings and 4) other images. This division was made *after* the images had been coded and catalogued. It is intended to serve as no more than an organizational scheme.

FAVORABLE IMAGES ASSIGNED
TO THE MALE: EVIDENCE

*Intellect*

Under this category, we examined the frequency with which male characters in the PITB could be described as: intelligent, educated, brilliant, studious, scholarly, skillful, diplomatic, careful, introspective, philosophical, idealistic, wise, rational, clever, resourceful, smart, persuasive, achieving and innovative. The parenthesized numerals following an image represent its salience score.

Education, both formal and informal, appears as the hallmark of INTELLIGENT (31) male actors. Judges use BRILLIANT (14) but folksy methods to determine the truth in cases brought to their courts. EDUCATED (39) males pass the Indian Civil Services (ICS) examinations, scoring in the highest percentiles. A few males even fill the stereotype of the eccentric genius.

Many boys show promise of achievement, and relatives reinforce their positive self-images by expecting them to do well. Edison sets up a laboratory when he is eight years old. At age 14, C.V. Raman enters college where he devises and conducts experiments with little formal assistance from peers or teachers. STUDIOUS (11) males pass their examinations with honours and often win scholarships for higher studies. Though not exactly a scholar, even Don Quixote copiously reads knighthood adventures. Men not only read books, they write them. Various SCHOLARLY (18) males appear as prolific authors.

Almost no field is left with a dearth of SKILLFUL (18) males. Raja Ram Mohan Roy achieves proficiency in Bengali, Arabic and Persian at an incredibly early age. We meet many, skilled fighters. When sticky situations warrant the use of diplomacy, DIPLOMATIC (5) and CAREFUL (15) men appear as judges, administrators, researchers, reformers, etc. But this is not a group of mere careerists. Artists as well as scientists use their talent for noble ends. Comprehending the horrors of child labor, an inventor feels compelled to create a labor-saving device. A knowledgeable and perceptive guru counsels those in trouble.

While businessmen watch the market, buy low, sell high, and earn excellent profits, many authors and philosophers reject the commercialization of intellect as a poor substitute for the satis-

faction inherent in independent intellectual pursuits. INTROS-
PECTIVE (3) and PHILOSOPHICAL (3) males envision futuris-
tic solutions. Vivekananda attempts to rejuvenate Hinduism.
IDEALIST (12) males undertake esoteric adventures to answer
philosophical questions: A king seeking an answer to the question "Who is greater, a householder or a monk?", keeps up his
long and arduous search until his philosophical query is resolved.
Though holymen are usually depicted as WISE (30), the lessons
describe a number of laymen, like Prospero, who accumulate wisdom through introspection and experimentation. Many RATIO-
NAL (5) males subscribe to atheism and have a declared faith in
utilitarian, modern science.

CLEVER (38) males appear as gurus, con men, and political
leaders. Their strategies range from political coup d'etats to chea-
ting tourists. In the battle of wits fought between Duryodhan and
Pandavas, the trapped Pandavas escape Duryodhan's wax palace
by building tunnels and disguising themselves as Brahmins. Such
schemes are admired as evidence of talent, and their perpetra-
tors are presented as heroes. In the deeds of Tom Sawyer, this
plotting becomes not only admirable but also comic.

PERSUASIVE (2) males have a glib tongue to aid them in
bargaining. In crises demanding prompt resolution, RESOUR-
CEFUL (16) males act with unrelenting optimism. Each time the
sailors are marooned on an island, they eat what is easily available, make tools or weapons from items found on the ground,
and build shelters from indigenous materials. A SMART (24)
slave uses his wits to win freedom. A playwright quickly invents
a feint to prevent the intruder from killing him.

Success crowns the male achiever in a variety of other areas,
too small to serve as independent image categories but too significant to be totally ignored. We coded males in all such areas as
ACHIEVERS (50). The image "achiever" used here is purely
nominal, since actors excluded from this category are not non-
achievers.

A wide range of successful operatives appear in this category.
Grenfell develops a nation out of wilderness. Other aehievers
build cities, free people from oppressive rule, discover miracle
drugs. Male explorers are the first to cross the Northwest
Passage, first to scale Mount Everest. Success is also won in areas
outside one's regular occupation. Through will power and deter-

mination, a paralysis victim overcomes his handicap.

The INNOVATIVE (49) male is usually presented as breaking away from the dominant paradigm of his age. Louis Pasteur's pioneer work in inoculation opens a whole new branch of medicine. While some men examine the nature of forces emitted by the sun and planets, others harness light and gravity to construct sun dials, water clocks, windmills and airplanes. Many innovations are of a more temporal nature, usually engineered in response to an immediate crisis. Manu and his friends devise a clever plan to capture a burglar and alert the police. Trapped on an island, Sindbad the Sailor ties himself to the legs of a great bird and thus frees himself.

## Character

Under this grouping of male-favorable characteristics, we coded evidence on the following images: commanding, confident, strong, independent, proud, self-respecting, brave, determined, devoted, duteous, vigilant, hardworking, persevering, politically activist, patriotic, oratorical, civic-spirited, liberal, universalistic, peaceloving, religious, secular, ambitious, competitive, disciplinarian, adventurous, tall, handsome, beautiful, agile, inspirational, respected, popular, accommodating, friendly, cheerful, humorous, loyal, earnest, generous, noble, humanitarian, self-sacrificing, humble, simple, honest, thankful, innocent, just, hospitable, polite, classicist, patient, cultured, gallant, protective and romantic.

The male's near-monopoly on leadership is one of the world's oldest and most pervasive stereotypes. Decisive and commanding women are accused, with or without a grudging degree of admiration, of becoming masculine. In our plots, COMMANDING (28) men lead in homes and on battlefields. Be it the era of tribal chiefs or the revolutionary turmoil of the twentieth century, politics and government emerge as arenas for the male to command. Men appear to be most CONFIDENT (15) when buoyed with a vision of their country's future or of their own competence. Various male Indian political leaders confidently envision a new and happier India.

Strength, another hallmark of masculinity, distinguishes the STRONG (54) male from the "weaker" sex. Males stalk the texts as creatures strong of limb and hard of muscle. Bhim,

Duryodhana, Nala, Satyavan and Bharat all are described as strong. When physically fragile, males are taunted into developing their physique. Naline, a flabby boy, develops his body to the muscularity befitting a man. In a plot involving the trials and tribulations of a new school teacher, both the teacher and his competitor are strong fighters who resolve the issue of dominance in a boxing match. Ram weds Sita because he is able to lift the bow others have failed to budge.

Since the texts expect the strong to die to save the weak, the strength of males extends beyond the brawn of their muscles. It is also the core of their character. More than one character resists the temptation of accepting a bribe. Scores of freedom fighters hold onto their convictions despite life imprisonment and deportation. Guru Nanak, when arrested by the soldiers of Babar, remains unaffected by the impending prospect of death. Common men step forward as disciples in the initiatory rites of Khalsa *panth*, fully aware that failure means death. INDEPENDENT (15) Subhash Bose forms his own political group after disagreeing with Congressional leadership. Mansur, the philosopher, propagates doctrine of atheistic self-assertion and is hanged for it. PROUD (21) males often manifest themselves in similar rituals of honor-or-death. Loath to compromise their principles, SELF-RESPECTING (12) males, proud of their work and chosen missions, hold themselves in high esteem. When the British prosecute Tilak for his nationalist editorials, he refuses to apologize to the British government and chooses jail instead. An Indian scientist who refuses to accept lower pay than his British colleagues lives in deep poverty for three years but wins wage parity in the end.

The texts are so filled with situations where men are BRAVE (82) and unflinching that one begins to wonder if there is anything left for women to do. Whether they fight in wars in the European theater or the numerous battles on the plains of India, the male soldiers project valorous images. The list of intrepid warrior is long. Accompaning bravery is loyalty to higher ideals in the face of danger. Jesus and Socrates refuse to give up their preaching and accept death. Martin Luther condemns the church's corruption and opposes papal exploitation of innocent believers.

In more than one instance, LOYAL (24) soldiers, generals, ministers, servants and slaves go to extremes to prove their fidelity. Birbal, the minister, is willing to die to protect his master's interests. Chand Bardai's loyalty to the imprisoned King Prithviraj might cost him his head, but the threat of death seldom dims the virtue of standing by one's friends. On seeing that his friend, a commoner, is about to be beaten up, the EARNEST (6) emperor of China himself jumps over the wall to join in the scuffle.

Although military men are most often forced to face death, men in other occupations class with the Fourth Horseman as well. Often nature is cast as the adversary of DETERMINED (29) males. Captain Oates walks to his death in the snow to save his fellow explorers. Columbus wagers his life against an uncharted ocean. Such daring is not limited to adult males. Sons often strive to emulate their fathers' standards of bravery. The narrator of of one lesson learns not to fear the war when his father goes off to fight. One young boy climbs to the top of a church spire and then completes the more perilous descent unscathed. It is little surprise that he goes on to be a valiant naval commander,

Historical figures animated in stories of DEVOTED (14) males. Even as college students, various Indians join the nationalist cause instead of enlisting in the comfortable ranks of civil servants. Once out of college, these men undertake massive social reform. VIGILANT (2) and DUTEOUS (13) males display both a sense of self-respect and an awareness of responsibility to community. As agents of the law, policemen are willing to die in defense of the public good, and will not hide from arrogant bullies and angry crowds.

In the categories of PATIENT (14), HARDWORKING (44) and PERSEVERING (21) males, we find men whose efforts are not always immediately recognized and rewarded. The texts are strewn with characters who build empires with nothing but the sweat of their steady effort. AMBITIOUS (15), COMPETITIVE (2), DISCIPLINED (9) and ADVENTUROUS (48) males seek immortality, achieve fame and inspire others.

Not all successful males are physically attractive but, numerous TALL (5) HANDSOME (19), BEAUTIFUL (1) and AGILE (4) male characters suggest a powerful correlation between success and physical attributes. In myths and modern stories alike, virtuous young men appear with well-built bodies and handsome faces. Complementing their good looks are attractive clothes, a smiling composure, erect posture and a charming disposition. The INSPIRATIONAL (2) male serves as a spring of spiritual strength.

Honored and RESPECTED (10) for their enlightening role, such males may also emerge as POPULAR (75) opinion leaders.

The agitator role seems to dominate the category for POLITICAL ACTIVISTS (29) and PATRIOTS (14). Powerful ORATORS (8) sway the masses. CIVIC-SPIRITED (24) Vinoba starts the *Bhooduan* movement to enlist voluntary contributions of land for people who have none. Many good male citizens uphold and abide by the law. Socrates, proponent of the doctrine of common good, acknowledges the authority of the law when he accepts the court's judgment that he should die. JUST (10) Mahabir Prasad Dwivedi refuses to use his position as an editor to promote social climbers who promise him money. Like UNIVERSALISTS (1), the LIBERAL (11) males oppose petty factionalism, while PEACELOVING (10) males strive for non-violent coexistence. Though devoted to their faiths, most RELIGIOUS (15) males are capable of transcending their religious loyalties. The SECULAR (4) males believe in Hindu-Muslim unity and reject religious bigotry.

The texts are full of GENEROUS (40) kings who help the needy and forgive their unfair critics. The generosity of poor men is even more admirable. A peasant farmer does not curse whosoever stole his breakfast. Instead he hopes that it does the thief some good. A similar selfless empathy distinguishes a number of NOBLE (30), HUMANITARIAN (17) males. Lincoln strives to abolish slavery; Robin Hood robs rich to help the poor; Akbar condemns sectarian parochialism; Ashoka aims to provide all animate beings with security and Joy. SELF-SACRIFICING (24) Telemachus steps between gladiators in an arena, and gives his life to stop the fight.

The texts describe various males as HUMBLE (26), SIMPLE (24), HONEST (32) THANKFUL (7) and INNOCENT (4). On receiving the Nobel Prize, Fleming modestly remarks that he did nothing but discover an obvious remedy. Dr Rajendra Prasad is portrayed as a simple man who leads an almost ascetic life even when surrounded by the amenities available to him as the president of a nation. Righteous males perform moral acts with no consideration of personal profit. When angels ask Bhoj if he ever coveted wealth and power, he replies in the affirmative, even though an honest answer is very likely to cost him the cherished throne of Vikramaditya.

A spirit of cooperation prompts ACCOMMODATING (18) and FRIENDLY (13) males. Boys seem especially able to conjure up the magic of friendship. The lessons showcase fun-loving, carefree, CHEERFUL (15) and lively boys. Good humor and a jovial nature distinguish the HUMOROUS (6) male. Whether they are old friends or merely strangers, HOSPITABLE (16) males treat their guests with warmth and courtesy. CLASSICIST (1), POLITE (6) and CULTURED (14) gentlemen employ social graces and cultivated speech. PROTECTIVE (3) and GALLANT (10) males protect women, whether they are princesses or homegrown sweethearts. A ROMANTIC (4) at heart, the gallant male pursues his love affairs with a tender sentimentality. Jamadar Lahna Singh promises his childhood sweetheart that he will protect her husband who is his immediate superior in the army. He keeps his promise and in so doing, loses his own life.

*Feelings*

In this grouping we have included the evidence for the following male-favourable images: loving, compassionate, kind and gentle.

The LOVING (20) male often appears as a devoted father, friend, husband, son, relative or companion. In secondary group settings, most COMPASSIONATE (34) males appear as strong but sensitive individuals who either try to solve problems of oppression and religious persecution, or aid victims of these social problems. At the primary group level, male characters accept responsibility for their loved ones, show concern for the aged, and safeguard their kin's welfare. The Nobel Prize winning biochemist, Hargovind Khurana, lives frugally on his scholarship funds while studying in England so that he can send money home to help his brother with family expenses.

Though gentleness is not stereotyped as a male characteristic, we do come across a few positive images of males who are GENTLE (6) and softspoken. The texts, however, abound with KIND (51) males. Employers, strangers and gods extend their kindness to the destitute. When a king is given the opportunity to save his own life by sacrificing a boy, he tells ministers that he would rather die than cause the death of another. The kindness of males extends to animals as well. To spare a deer, Buddha offers his own body as game to a hunter.

This summarizes the evidence on male-favorable images in our sample. After a similar presentation of the evidence for female-favorable images, we shall compare the male and female images to verify our hypothesis. Table 2 lists, in a descending order of frequency, the favorable images counted for the male.

### FAVORABLE IMAGES ASSIGNED TO THE FEMALE: EVIDENCE

We organized evidence for the female-favorable images under the same system used for the male-favorable images.

*Intellect*

A highly revered and frequently mentioned image in Indian mythology is the image of Saraswati—the goddess of learning. EDUCATED (14) women appear as erudite and conversant in current affairs. Sarojini Naidu, a child prodigy, passes her high school examination at the age of eleven. Laxmi Bai is trained in the art of handling arms, horseback riding and warfare. SCHOLARLY (3) Princess Jahanara delves in diplomacy, and writes religious commentaries. Her brothers seek her advice on matters of state.

Well-traveled, WISE (3), INTELLIGENT (5) females appear familiar with the ways of the world. When Budhimati's husband, the king's minister, doesn't come home, she concludes that something terrible must have happened. A keen observer, she discovers where her husband is by listening to a group of water-carriers along the road. She sneaks through the city gate to the prison tower, consults with him and successfully carries out his plan for escape.

As ACHIEVERS (6) females excel in a number of fields. Marie Curie wins the Nobel Prize. INNOVATIVE (10) women find original solutions to their problems. When Queen Karmavati is outnumbered by her enemies, she sends a *raakhi* to the Mughal king, Humayun, who is at war with most of the Rajput states.

Impressed by the uniqueness of her DIPLOMATIC (1) approach, Humayun comes to her aid.

In most situations, however, the females' intellect seems turned toward resolving problems of their households, personal affairs, and love lives. A young girl outsmarts her father to avoid a

TABLE 2

*List of Favorable Images Assigned to the Male Descending Order of Frequency*

| Frequency | Images | Frequency | Images |
|---|---|---|---|
| 82 | Brave | 14 | Patriotic |
| 75 | Popular | 13 | Duteous |
| 54 | Strong | 13 | Faithful |
| 51 | Kind | 13 | Friendly |
| 50 | Achiever | 12 | Idealist |
| 49 | Innovative | 12 | Self-respecting |
| 48 | Adventurous | 11 | Liberal |
| 44 | Hard-working | 11 | Studious |
| 40 | Generous | 10 | Gallant |
| 39 | Educated | 10 | Heroic |
| 38 | Clever | 10 | Just |
| 34 | Compassionate | 10 | Peace-loving |
| 32 | Honest | 10 | Respected |
| 31 | Intelligent | 9 | Disciplinarian |
| 30 | Noble | 8 | Orator |
| 30 | Wise | 7 | Thankful |
| 29 | Determined | 6 | Earnest |
| 29 | Political Activist | 6 | Gentle |
| 28 | Commanding | 6 | Humorous |
| 26 | Humble | 6 | Polite |
| 24 | Civic Spirited | 5 | Diplomatic |
| 24 | Loyal | 5 | Rational |
| 24 | Self-sacrificing | 5 | Tall |
| 24 | Simple | 4 | Agile |
| 24 | Smart | 4 | Innocent |
| 21 | Persevering | 4 | Romantic |
| 21 | Proud | 4 | Secular |
| 20 | Loving | 3 | Introspective |
| 19 | Handsome | 3 | Philosophic |
| 18 | Accommodating | 3 | Practical |
| 18 | Scholarly | 3 | Protective |
| 18 | Skillful | 2 | Competitive |
| 17 | Humanitarian | 2 | Divine |
| 16 | Hospitable | 2 | Inspirational |
| 16 | Resourceful | 2 | Persuasive |
| 15 | Ambitious | 2 | Saintly |
| 15 | Careful | 2 | Spiritualist |
| 15 | Cheerful | 2 | Vigilant |
| 15 | Confident | 1 | Aristocratic |
| 15 | Independent | 1 | Beautiful |
| 15 | Religious | 1 | Big |
| 14 | Brilliant | 1 | Classicist |
| 14 | Cultured | 1 | Immortality Seeker |
| 14 | Devoted | 1 | Universalist |
| 14 | Patient | | |

marriage of convenience. BRILLIANT (2) Panna Dhaai creates a foolproof plan which saves the life of her ward. CLEVER (8) Savitri outwits Yama, the god of death, and saves her husband's life. SMART (3) Portia not only saves Antonio's life, but also procures Bassanvio's ring so that, once home, she can reveal her true identity and relish the fruits of her courtroom victory.

CAREFUL (3), PRACTICAL (2) women take a realistic approach to the problems of household budgeting. PERSUASIVE (1) Florence Nightingale makes her family agree to let her study nursing in Paris. SKILLFUL (7) Yupi is the King's favorite dancer. An AGILE (8) grandmother takes control at the onset of a fire and handles the crisis coolly.

*Character*

Tha texts present various AMBITIOUS (5) and ADVEN-TUROUS (4) females. Sarojini Naidu's ambition enables her to become a great poet and a successful politician in an era when most of India's women were confined to their homes. One girl aspires to attend school and receive an education usually reserved for males. A princess, bored with the life of the palace, dresses herself as a commoner and sneaks out to seek adventure.

Females tend to be INDEPENDENT (14) most often in the home. Their handling of in-law problems, commonly cited in the texts, indicate the level of woman's autonomy. A housewife, who has been rejected by her in-laws because she is of a lower caste, will not ask them for help while her husband is sick. With no assistance, she nurses her husband back to health.

Outside the home, COMMANDING (5) women like Laxmi Bai and Karmavati guide war preparations and command in the battlefields. Indira Gandhi learns a great deal in and out of her household about the complexities of statecraft, and she demonstrates a sure-footed independence in politics.

Women, STRONG (6) in body and character, stand their ground. Glenda swims for 20 hours with nothing to keep her afloat, except her physical strength. Sarojini, stronger and healthier than her flabby husband, inspires him to follow a body-building routine to develop a stronger physique. CONFIDENT (3) Jija Bai firmly believes that the rumors of her son's death are false. A PATIENT (5) housewife suffers the extravagance of her uninvited guests with good humor. HUMANITARIAN (4) women extend themselves in a FRIENDLY (6) and encouraging manner, while HUMOROUS (4) and CHEERFUL (7) women appreciate levity even in chaotic situations. Aunt Maria mildly suggests to Uncle Podger that the next time he goes to hammer a nail in the wall, he should inform her ahead of time so that she can arrange to spend a week with her mother.

SIMPLE (2) women live unpretentiously, taking delight in the ordinary gifts of nature—honey, flowers and wild fruits. Many follow ascetic, religious routines. JUST (2), NOBLE (8), HONEST (4) women practice and defend truth. A housewife argues forcefully with her husband against accepting a bribe. She even asks the police officer to arrest her husband. Acting as a DISCIPLINARIAN (1), Aunt Maria will not allow her children to hear abusive language.

Matters of integrity, personal and ancestral pride, or issues related to tradition, appear as some of the focal concerns of IDEALIST (5) females. An upright wife of a literary critic scolds her husband for prostituting his artistic integrity to make money. She succeeds in making him adhere to his ideals of ascetic scholarship. In more than one instance, the texts enhance the female's image as a DIVINE (1) INSPIRATIONAL (3) and HOLY (2) personage, whose virtues surpass those of goddesses and saints. PROUD (9) of their venerable qualities, SELF-RESPECTING (3) females draw their strength from accomplishments in and outside the home. A young widow refuses to be bullied by the local Romeos. Madhoolika, a poor farmer proud of her ancestral heritage, declines the King's lucrative offer to buy her land.

The bravery of females manifests itself more in resistance than in aggression. BRAVE (23) women endure hardships, deal with murderers' threats and survive the abuses dealt by cruel in-laws. As PATRIOTIC (4), POLITICAL ACTIVISTS (12), females participate in movements for social change. They join the satyagrah movement, spin *khaadi*, donate personal jewelry for political funds and manage families while their husbands serve time in prison for opposing the British rule. An effective ORATOR (1), Sarojini Naidu travels all over the country to organize people to fight for the nationalist cause. Broad-minded and LIBERAL (1), she also marries out of her caste. Touched by the needs of famine victims, a CIVIC-SPIRITED (7) lower-middle-class housewife persuades her husband to make a hefty contribution to the relief fund.

The lessons depict various women who toil in and out of the home. More than one HARD-WORKING (19) widow is shown struggling to feed her children. PERSEVERING (5) women refuse to be discouraged. A mother, searching for her son, unwaveringly visits every street, stops at every crowd and spends Sundays in front of the churches.

DEVOTED (10) and DUTEOUS (4) women consecrate every effort to follow their beliefs. Kasturba seldom contradicts her husband and believes such absolute obedience to be the main virtue of an Indian wife. Princesses and queens leave their palaces without hesitation to follow their husbands into the forests. While males swear their allegiance to their country or profess devotion to higher ideals, women prove themselves FAITHFUL (19) by being *pativrataas*, loyal and obedient to their husbands. The LOYAL (17) female expresses fidelity, love, gratitude and above all, a strong bond of allegiance to her kith and kin. Only Panna Dhaai is true to her employer in a marketplace situation. Most other females endure hardships, suffering, even rejection to support their spouses with resolute allegiance. As an ultimate demonstration of such fealty, a housewife ardently states that a woman should be willing to sacrifice her life for her husband. And true to form, the Indian textbooks show Rajput widows committing *jauhar* to remain loyal to their dead husbands.

An ability to change her own viewpoint in order to avoid conflict appears as the predominant characteristic of the ACCOMMODATING (10) woman. Many a RELIGIOUS (9) woman prays on her knees for the safety of her spouse. The GENEROUS (17) and HOSPITABLE (13) woman is kind to all guests. Mamta, a princess turned peasant, shelters the deposed Mughal King who has killed her father and forced her into exile. In doing so, she is following her *dharma*, the Indian tradition of offering hospitality to all who seek shelter. Other generous women go to SELF-SACRIFICING (13) extremes. Della willingly sacrifices her one beautiful possession, her hair, in order to buy her husband a decent Christmas present.

BEAUTIFUL (42) princesses, housewives, maidens and slave-girls parade throughout the texts. Parents appear anxious whether their daughter will grow up to be pretty. INNOCENT (3), PROPITIOUS (2) and CULTURED (9) females are presented for admiration. Propitious females are often compared with Laxmi, the goddess of wealth. Cultured females articulate their views with a well-mannered eloquence. Miss Holmes debates the propriety of India's right to freedom with her father. A housewife displays her cultural awareness by knowing the proper styles of furniture and flashy trend-setters.

*Feelings*

Under this section, we compiled evidence for the following female-favorable images: kind, loving, protective, compassionate and motherly.

Females of every generation are credited with KIND (23) acts. Tender care is what children often remember of their mothers. Daughters seem to have a special sympathy for their fathers' troubles. Princes Jahanara shares the sufferings of her father as she cares for him in his old age. Women often take pity on wounded animals as well.

On limited occasions, the compassion of females supersedes domestic matters. A housewife, who believes the servant has been falsely accused because he is poor, defends his innocence. But as a general rule, the LOVING (20) woman's affection is directed towards two of her most important life forces: her husband and her children. PROTECTIVE (6) and concerned, Sona insists on keeping the rent money in order to buy a blanket for her husband in the winter. One of a woman's functions is maintaining the health of male characters. COMPASSIONATE (18) wives nurse their sick husbands, while MOTHERLY (5) women act as guardian angels to their dear ones. Mothers are shown as particularly adept at feeding the ambitions as well as the stomachs of people in their household. While Marconi's mother worries about him staying up late every night, she understands his need to work so diligently and continually encourages him. Another mother allows her daughter to invite friends over. When 50 girls arrive in response to the invitation, she does not scold her daughter. Instead, she tells her daughter to stop crying and assures her that they will manage to feed everyone. (Note that while this buttercup is shown crying Marconi and other boys of her age are shown studying intricate problems.)

Table 3 lists, in a descending order of frequencies, the favorable images counted for the female.

TABLE 3

*List of Favorable Images Assigned to the Female
Descending Order of Frequency*

| Frequency | Images | Frequency | Images |
|---|---|---|---|
| 42 | Beautiful | 5 | Persevering |
| 23 | Brave | 4 | Adventurous |
| 23 | Kind | 4 | Duteous |
| 20 | Loving | 4 | Honest |
| 19 | Faithful | 4 | Humanitarian |
| 19 | Hardworking | 4 | Humorous |
| 18 | Compassionate | 4 | Patriotic |
| 17 | Generous | 4 | Respected |
| 17 | Loyal | 3 | Affectionate |
| 14 | Educated | 3 | Careful |
| 14 | Independent | 3 | Confident |
| 13 | Determined | 3 | Innocent |
| 13 | Hospitable | 3 | Inspirational |
| 13 | Self-sacrificing | 3 | Scholarly |
| 12 | Political Activist | 3 | Self-respecting |
| 10 | Accommodating | 3 | Smart |
| 10 | Devoted | 3 | Wise |
| 10 | Innovative | 2 | Brilliant |
| 10 | Popular | 2 | Holy |
| 9 | Cultured | 2 | Just |
| 9 | Proud | 2 | Practical |
| 9 | Religious | 2 | Propitious |
| 8 | Agile | 2 | Simple |
| 8 | Clever | 1 | Artistic |
| 8 | Noble | 1 | Child prodigy |
| 7 | Cheerful | 1 | Diplomatic |
| 7 | Civic spirited | 1 | Disciplinarian |
| 7 | Skillful | 1 | Divine |
| 6 | Achiever | 1 | Earnest |
| 6 | Friendly | 1 | Gentle |
| 6 | Protective | 1 | Humble |
| 6 | Strong | 1 | Liberal |
| 5 | Ambitious | 1 | Orator |
| 5 | Commanding | 1 | Peace-loving |
| 5 | Idealist | 1 | Persuasive |
| 5 | Intelligent | 1 | Poetic |
| 5 | Motherly | 1 | Serious |
| 5 | Patient | 1 | Thankful |

## MALE- AND FEMALE-FAVORABLE IMAGES:
### A COMPARISON

While coding, we counted both the favorable and unfavorable images for the male and female characters in our lessons. We have analyzed in detail, however, only the favorable images. In the following discussion, we have cited the frequency of unfavorable images only for the purposes of comparison. Unlike the evidence for favorable images, evidence for unfavorable images in not reported for a methodological reason. An unfavorable image was not always found to be the exact antonym of the corresponding favorable image. Our comparison of favorable and unfavorable images is quantitative, dealing only with the total frequency counts. Also, since all percentages have been rounded to the nearest whole number, some column totals throughout the book may exceed the expected total of one hundred.

While examining the distribution of the total image count, it should be noted that the original sex composition of the total cast of PITB characters reflected a 4:1 male-female ratio. But by our methodology, even when an image referring to members of a particular sex occurred more than once in a lesson, it was listed only once for that lesson. Thus the exact proportion of male and female characters in a lesson might not be reflected in the image-count.

Despite this limitation, when we used the 4:1 male-female ratio as a heuristic device for comparative purposes, we discovered that the PITB reflect a pronounced bias in the distribution of both favorable and unfavorable images to the female and male characters. We counted a total of 2,074 favorable images in the texts (Table 4). The females, constituting 20% of the total characters in the PITB, received 25% of the favorable images. The distribution for unfavorable images, however, decisively offsets the 5% gain scored by the females in favorable images. The females (20%) received 34% of the unfavorable images, while the male (80%) received only 66% of the unfavorable images. Table 5 confirmed this uneven treatment of the female. The PITB may not have handicapped the female by lowering her share of the favorable images, but she was definitely assigned a higher share of the unfavorable images.

Neither lesson-origin nor language appeared as significant

TABLE 4

*Total Favorable and Unfavorable Images
By Sex of Characters in the PITB*

| Images | Character's Sex | | Total |
| | Men | Women | |
|---|---|---|---|
| Favorable | 75% | 25% | 100% (2074) |
| Unfavorable | 66% | 34% | 100% (869) |

Chi-square = 24.5
df = 1
Level of Significance = .001

TABLE 5

*Male and Female Characters in the PITB By Total
Favorable and Unfavorable Images
Assigned to Them*

| Images | Character's Sex | |
| | Men | Woman |
|---|---|---|
| Favorable | 73% | 64% |
| Unfavorable | 27% | 36% |
| Total | 100% (2125) | 100% (818) |

Chi-square = 24.5
= 1
Level of Significance = .001

variables in the distribution of favorable images.[1] In Table 6, the sex of the author seemed to make a noticeable, but not conclusive, difference in the composition of sex role imagery. In lessons written by female authors, the percentage of both favorable and unfavourable images was higher for women appearing as characters, than it was for men. From the distributions in Table 6, it is possible to suggest that the inclusion of a greater number of female authors might lead to an increase in the number of lessons with sex role imagery favorable to women. However, since Table 6 also indicated that even female authors describe women unfavorably more often than not, any increase in favorable imagery would be offset by an equal rise in the proportion on unfavorable images assigned to women by female authors. In view of these contractory indications, it is difficult to judge the

TABLE 6

*Favorable & Unfavorable Images Assigned to*
*Male & Female Characters, by Author's Sex*

| | Character's Sex | | | |
| | Favorable Images | | Unfavorable Images | |
| Author's Sex | Men | Women | Men | Women |
|---|---|---|---|---|
| Male | 66% | 58% | 71% | 52% |
| Female | 10% | 24% | 10% | 30% |
| Male & Female | 1% | 0% | 1% | 1% |
| Indeterminable | 24% | 18% | 18% | 17% |
| | 100% | 100% | 100% | 100% |
| | (1547) | (578) | (527) | (291) |

impact of author's sex on the nature of sex role imagery in the
PITB.

*Male and Female Favorable Images: Discussion*

In one of the few self-concept studies done in India, George
and Mathews (1967), found that the ideal self-concept of the
Indian man was to be courageous and free from vices, while the
Indian woman idealized her self-concept as being humble, loving
and free from jealousy.

Which of these images do the textbooks present?

A glimpse of the ten images with the highest salience scores
in Tables 2 and 3 shows the following images to be common to
both sexes: Brave, Kind, Hardworking, Generous and Educated.
These common images are assets in both marketplace and non-
marketplace contexts and do not highlight any significant difference in sex role characterization. However, the bias toward
characterizing the male for marketplace success is pronounced
in the images *not* found among the top ten of the female list. The
male is assigned Popular, Strong, Achiever, Innovative and
Adventurous, all images comparatively more conducive to
marketplace success than non-marketplace roles. In the two image
lists, the male scores highest as "brave" while the female list is
topped by "beautiful." Images assigned exclusively to the female
at the top-ten level include Beautiful, Loving, Faithful, Compassionate and Loyal, all distinctively more suited to success in non-
marketplace situations.

One exception to the above mode of distribution occurs with the appearance of "political activist" in the top ten images for the female in Hindi lesson of Indian origin. This, however, can be explained by the high concentration of female subjects of biography in this category, many of whom were important political figures.

There are so many differences, implicit and explicit, in the activities assigned to the two sexes that even common images project differentiated role models, generally hampering the image of the female. Given the range of their activities, we coded many females as "commanding." But the texts present no administrative hierarchy in which even a respectable number of staff members are female. A queen's administrative staff, from ministers to soldiers, is generally composed of men. Often the queen occupies the throne only after her husband's death or when he is off adventuring or fighting wars. Reviewing the cast of characters, one searches in vain for women who are secure enough in their power to grant freedom to an enemy or a servant, an act casually performed by many men.

Women pushing for advancement in these texts run a much higher risk of failure than men. While males can enjoy success in their work and comfort at home, the female characters, like the dancer Yupi, must choose between career and family. Neelu, a college lecturer, exemplifies the ambivalence of females who marry after a successful professional career. They do not quite know whether to slip into the expected housewife routines or continue their professional interests. After marriage, Neelu gives up college teaching. Shrinivas, her husband, congratulates her for running the house, thus freeing him to run his business with undivided attention. After some time, Neelu is piqued when a colleague publishes an article on a topic she herself had suggested. Neelu makes a feeble attempt to get back into research, but this gesture to resume her pre-marriage professional interest seems little more than symbolic. To the reader, the message is unmistakable. A female may work hard, get a job and succeed before marriage, but marriage is a dead end for a research-oriented female. Marriage as an institution does not permit the wife to continue her intellectual pursuits. She must play a subordinate hostess role, adjusting her ambition to the priorities of her husband's occupational goals.

Many females with regular outside jobs perform chores with judicious attention to household maintenance. Other than the subjects of biographies, the ordinary female character in the PITB does not explore new frontiers of knowledge. Rambha is portrayed as a highly intelligent and resourceful woman, yet she is never confronted with problems common to the man's world of work and achievement. All her crises are rooted in romance. Her first struggle is triggered by her desire to escape marriage to a money bag. Her second crisis stems from her desire to turn her romance with the prince into marriage. She never demonstrates any inclination to learn a trade or enter an occupation. Even though she is intelligent and tough, her concept of success is synonymous with marriage to a good man.

When women do exert power, their activities are either regulated by males, or are dependent upon the male-dominant normative structure. Kasturba is politically active, but her strength of character is measured according to the orthodox female stereotype. While men act to stamp out injustice by relieving suffering, heroines are considered successful if they can manage to maintain the status quo. In virtually every case, hardworking males can expect their industry to be rewarded with all the trappings of success. On the other hand, females work diligently with little hope of advancement in their financial status or prestige. The most pressing (depressing?) example of this inequality is the lot of housewives, whose countless chores are rarely considered worthwhile labor. Still they work conscientiously, slaving to prepare great feasts and to maintain their often slothful spouses. In a lesson, the mother who comes home to find her daughters hard at work cleaning the kitchen in the middle of the afternoon comments that females should be trained while they are young to accept these chores as their destiny.

The aspiration that sons be formally educated is common in the texts. Such family ambitions, rarely, if ever, apply to daughters. Women, in general, are not presented as being nearly as well-educated as men. The contents of some lessons leave the impression that only males are capable of learning skills. A shopkeeper hopes that one of his sons will take over when he dies. The possibility of a daughter doing so is never mentioned.

The texts credit few females with enough confidence to formulate a national or scientific vision, much less to make that vision a reality. The males are always shown to be more farsighted, self-assured and public-spirited. As in virtually every favorable category, the instances of persevering females fall short of the number and variety of occasions in which males persevere. While many men challenge the awesome might of nature, few ep isodes involve women struggling with primordial forces. Helen Keller is the only female character called to overcome her physical limitations with the strength of her will. Madame Curie's experimentation and success provide only a slight counterbalance to the steadfast research done by many male characters.

The beautiful woman's power to inspire the male is, at best, a passive attribute. However, in the parallel male category, physical beauty is often linked to an active nobleness and spiritual beauty. The only moral value even vaguely related to feminine beauty is faithfulness. This is fitting since attractive features are supposed to render a girl more suitable for marriage. While many women are faithful to their husbands, very few male characters are portrayed as devoted to their wives except in romantic melodrama. At times the degree of a woman's reverence for her husband's wisdom reaches ludicrous levels. For years, Anandi remains faithful to her husband Shankar—an unemployed alcoholic. When Nala loses his kingdom by gambling, Damayanti follows him into the forest, insisting that a faithful wife could not leave her husband. Nala deserts her in the forest, proving that Damayanti's loyalty is no match for her husband's power to decide what is best for them. It is interesting to note that such discretionary power, at the cost of a woman's happiness, is assigned to a male who has just gambled his kingdom away. If the lessons are to be believed, every woman must swear her total allegiance to a male, regardless of the merit.

The behavior coded as motherly further illustrates the point. The texts imply that it is the natural order for women to bear, and care for, children. In the episode of the barren aunt, the woman's life is not deemed complete until she finds a substitute for the children she herself cannot bring into the world.

Describing her accommodating disposition, Mrs Tulliver uses the term "obedient" to describe her niece Lucy Deane, who is the same age as her daughter Maggie. Lucy is a good girl, who, when told to sit on a chair, does so for as long as an hour without a murmur or resentment. Such passivity would be considered unhealthy in a boy. Males prove their resilience in the classroom, in the marketplace, on the battlefield and in countless other situations. Unexposed to such situations, women are taught to adjust to domestic problems. No wonder Lucy is praised for being passive.

In socially amicable relationships, women are seldom equal to men. They can encourage male achievement, but they do not participate as equal partners. At best, they act as helpers. The art of gentle and sympathetic consolation which young females learn from their mothers and grandmothers serves them well when they enter traditionally female occupations such as nursing and teaching. Except for Florence Nightingale and Miss Beam who remain single, most females in the PITB end up being married. In their own households, they uphold the gentle support system that for generations has supplied encouragement and shelter to ambitious males. Maintaining such a system is highly time-consuming and constraining. The female is rarely given the opportunity to practise kindness far from her own neighbourhood, much less to travel from village to village preaching doctrines as some males do. The texts portray women as compassionate. Still, the task of restructuring society so that discrimination, religious persecution, inequality, and other deep-rooted ills are eradicated is generally left to the virulent outrage of men.

Among female characters coded as generous, a school principal is the only one who can give more than jewels, cash or hospitality. She travels outside the city and across a river to bring knowledge to poor village children. But even her efforts appear puny compared to the great male teachers who deal in reorienting the lifestyles of an entire nation.

Both males and females appear as self-sacrificing characters. But once the supporting evidence for the different images is sorted, it appears that women have no female friends worthy of their self-sacrifice. Women suffer only for men. As if women were incapable of formulating ideals on their own, most often, their sacrifices are not dictated by chosen conviction, but by traditional duties assigned to wives and mothers. The only instances of women losing their lives for others are recorded when wives fling themselves on the burning pyres of their husbands. These are dramatic but futile gestures of loyalty—the husbands remain dead. Male characters sacrifice their lives so that others may live.

In the beginning of this chapter, we had hypothesized:

H-1. As compared to the traditional literary stereotypes, the sex role imagery in the PITB will portray the members of both the sexes as whole human beings and not merely in terms of their traditional, stereotypic, masculine-feminine attributes.

In biographies and other lessons, the PITB present us with male and female achievers. There are various female characters who gain prestige and popularity for qualities other than their beauty or sex appeal. But they are few and far between. Confronted with a preponderance of male achievement imagery, the readers are likely to perceive female achievements as accidents. The PITB do not really portray the members of both sexes as whole human beings, independent of the stereotype sex role attributes.

Hypothesis 1 is rejected.

### FOOTNOTES

[1]The levels of significance in chi-square tests for Tables 7 and 8 are low but signifactory. Since half the texts in our sample are prescribed by Rajasthan and U.P., roughly half the male-female favourable images seem to fall in the categories for these two agencies. Holding sex constant in Table 9, we find no significant differences in the distribution within the categories of male and female favorable images by agency, grade level, origins and language. A total of 38% of the male-favourable images occur

### TABLE 7

#### FAVORABLE IMAGES, SEX BY LESSON ORIGIN

| Lesson's Origin | Character's Sex | |
|---|---|---|
| | Male | Female |
| Indian | 56% | 58% |
| Non-Indian | 44% | 42% |
| | 100% | 100% |
| | (1545) | (529) |

Chi-square=.69
df=1
Level of significance=.5

in the biographies, while only 28% of the female-favorable images occur in the biography category (Table 9). Since the non-biography type lessons represent 80% of the total lessons, the incidence of 38% male favorable images in the biography category represents a concentration that, once again, highlights the male as a significant achiever. The level of significance of chi-spuare test for Table 9 is high.

TABLE 8

### FAVORABLE IMAGES, SEX BY LANGUAGE

| Language | Character's Sex | |
| --- | --- | --- |
| | *Male* | *Female* |
| Hindi | 43% | 36% |
| English | 67% | 64% |
| | 100% | 100% |
| | (1547) | (527) |

Chi-suqare$=1.67$
df$=1$
Level of significance$=.2$

TABLE 9

### FAVORABLE IMAGES, SEX BY LESSON TYPE

| Lesson Type | *Male* | *Female* |
| --- | --- | --- |
| Biography | 38% | 28% |
| Non-Biography | 62% | 72% |
| | 100% | 100% |
| | (1547) | (527) |

Chi-square$=17.57$
df$=1$
Level of significance$=.001$

TABLE 10

FAVORABLE: SUMMARY TABLE

| | | Author's Sex | | | | |
|---|---|---|---|---|---|---|
| | *Male* | *Female* | *M & F* | *Anonymous* | *Indeterminable* | |
| Male | 66% | 10% | 1% | 8% | 16% | 100% (1547) |
| Female | 58% | 24% | .19% | 5% | 14% | 100% (527) |

| | | | Agency | | | | | |
|---|---|---|---|---|---|---|---|---|
| | Central Board | Har-yana | Kuruk-shetra | NCERT | Punjab | Rajas-than | U.P. | |
| Male | 12% | 6% | 10% | 11% | 7% | 29% | 26% | 100% (1547) |
| Female | 8% | 6% | 9% | 8% | 8% | 29% | 32% | 100% (527) |

| | Grade Level | | | |
|---|---|---|---|---|
| | High School | Higher Secondary | Pre-Univ. | |
| Male | 50% | 40% | 10% | 100% (1547) |
| Female | 46% | 45% | 9% | 100% (527) |

| | Lesson Type | | |
|---|---|---|---|
| | Biography | Non-Biography | |
| Male | 38% | 62% | 100% (1547) |
| Female | 28% | 72% | 100% (527) |

| | Origins | | |
|---|---|---|---|
| | Indian | Non-Indian | |
| Male | 56% | 44% | 100% (1547) |
| Female | 58% | 42% | 100% (527) |

| | Language | | |
|---|---|---|---|
| | Hindi | English | |
| Male | 33% | 67% | 100% (1547) |
| Female | 36% | 64% | 100% (527) |

# CHAPTER V

# Sex Ratio of Authors, Language and Anti-Feminism

In this chapter, we propose to test the following hypotheses related to the sex ratio of authors, male-centered language and anti-feminine statements in the PITB:

H-2. The number of male authors in the PITB will not be far higher than that of female authors.

H-3. As compared to the sexism of the traditional linguistic usage, the PITB will not use nouns or pronouns that exclude famales in generalizations about the human society or the world.

H-4. As compared to the predominantly negative role-image of the female in traditional literary sex role stereotypes, the PITB will not foster contempt for women by including anti-feminine statements that put down women in general as inferior.

## SEX RATIO OF THE LESSONS' AUTHORS

Males constitute the majority as authors/editors of PITB.[1] Two-third of the textbooks were edited or authored by males. In 17% of the textbooks, the sex of the author/editor was indeterminable. Ten per cent of the textbooks were authored/edited by males *and* females, while females appeared as author/editor for only 7% of the textbooks. In all three grade levels (high schools, higher secondary, pre-university) the males appeared as author/editor for 60% or more of the textbooks. In the language category, 70% of Hindi textbooks and 62% of the English textbooks were written by males.

In lessons, too, the male authors constituted a majority.

Among the total authors of 353 lessons, the males represented 75%, followed by 16% unknown authors and 9% female authors.

In the last three decades, there has been a tremendous growth in the literary output by female writers, both in India and abroad. We had generated H-2 hoping that fair proportion of the PITB would be authored by Indian women. But the editors of the PITB seem oblivious to the need to offset the traditional imbalance. The dismally low proportion of female authors is consistently sustained in all the categories of our sample. Hypothesis 2 is rejected.

## MALE-CENTERED LANGUAGE

Sexism in language asserts itself in an excessive usage of male-centered language. Male-centered language discriminates against women by identifying men *and* women only in masculine terms. For example, both Hindi and English languages use masculine terms and pronouns to denote male as well as female subjects.

To measure the extent of male-centered language, the lessons in our sample were read with attention to the usage of masculine nouns and pronouns as all-inclusive terms.

One-fifth of the lessons (N=70) in our sample contained explicit evidence of male-centered language. Most were stories (47%, N=33) and biographies (31%, N=22). Two-third of the lessons with male-centered language were written by males, while females had authored only 14% of them (Table 11).

TABLE 11

### LESSONS WITH MALE CENTERED LANGUAGE BY AUTHOR'S SEX

| Author's Sex | Lessons with Male Centered Language |
|---|---|
| Male | 63% (44) |
| Female | 14% (10) |
| Male & Female | 2% ( 1) |
| Indeterminable | 22% (15) |
| | 100% (70) |

A lesson's origin appeared to be a more crucial determinant

of its male-centeredness. Twenty-six percent of the total lessons with non-Indian plots contained male-centered language (Table 12). The level of significance in chi-square tests for Table 12 was not high but significant.

TABLE 12

LESSON'S LANGUAGE BY ORIGIN
LANGUAGE

| Origin | Male-Centered | Not Male-Centered | |
|---|---|---|---|
| Indian | 15% | 85% | 100% |
| | (29) | (168) | (197) |
| Non-Indian | 26% | 74% | 100% |
| | (40) | (114) | (154) |

Chi-square = 6.9
df = 1
Level of Significance = .01

A lesson's language emerged as the most important determinant of its male-centeredness. While only 5% (6) of all Hindi lessons displayed male-centered language, 28% (64) of the total lessons in English included such language. This meant that 91% (64) of the 70 lessons with male-centered language appeared in English textbooks (Table 13). The level of significance in the chi-square test for Table 13 was significantly high. Thus the lessons with non-Indian plots written in English by males appeared most likely to contain male-centered language.

TABLE 13

LESSONS WITH MALE-CENTERED LANGUAGE, BY
LESSON'S LANGUAGE

LANGUAGE

| Lesson's Language | Male Centered | Not Male-Centered | |
|---|---|---|---|
| Hindi | 5% | 95% | 100% |
| | (6) | (117) | (123) |
| English | 28% | 72% | 100% |
| | (64) | (166) | (230) |

Chi-square = 26.5
df = 1
Level of Significance = .001

*Evidence*

The PITB often use the word "man" and its variants to refer to people of both sexes. The words "man" and "men" are consistently used even where "people" or "human beings" would be appropriate. The word *purushaartha*, (man's labor) for example, is a definitely masculine term, wherein *purush* (the male) is the operant adjective term. Yet the PITB often use the term *purushaartha* to denote the endeavors of both males and females.

In English language lessons, too, the word "man" is consistently used as a substitute for "person," "individual," "people" or "someone." Stranded sailors look for any "signs of men" (22:21). An underground exploration shows "that prehistoric men had been at work in the passage. . ." (39:45). The description of a city reads, "men lived together. . .men helped each other" (05:32). The sea has a call for the males as "it has called so many sons of Norway through the centuries" (05:92). The word "man" represents all the citizens of Vaishali, males and females. Albert Einstein is informed by his uncle, an engineer, that "algebra is a lazy man's arithmetic" (17:28). In the "Essay on Duty," all strong people are treated as men: "The strong man dies as a soldier to save the weak women and children at home" (36:98). "England expects every man to do his duty" (36:71). In a lesson called "The Men Behind," the author describes the function of an army's backup forces, writing, "And how does each man know where to go?. . .there must be some men behind to arrange everything. . .for every fighting soldier there are at least four men behind. . ." (05:108). It does not even occur to the author that women also work behind the lines.

The collective noun "men" is used to refer to masses of men and women. While casting his beloved's bust, a sculptor remarks, "Men will remember my beautiful little Yupi for thousands of years" (05:31). Describing the process of education for boys and girls at the Tolstoy farm in South Africa, Gandhiji, as an author, does use terms like youngsters, children and once, "boys and girls" (16:42). But whenever it comes to discussing the specific problems of teaching, the "Father of the Indian Nation" reverts to the masculine gender (16:41). A story about Abraham Lincoln extolls "the chance of any little backwoods boy to become president of the United States" (18:61). Apparently backwoods girls are not in the running.

While referring to the human race, authors use the masculine gender to include both genders. "The Man in Asbestos," an allegory of the future, represents the "final victory of men and machinery" (L-164). The words "mankind" and "brotherhood" are used to signify the unity of all people, including women. Describing the scene of communal prayer on the morning of the Muslim festival Id, Prem Chand writes, "As if a link of brotherhood had joined all these souls in a trance" (12:10). The term "boys" is used to denote all the students in a co-educational school (15:02).

It is common for the authors in the PITB to begin with a general form and refer to it thereafter with a masculine pronoun. Pronouns of the masculine gender are often used to designate both men and women. "Each Lapp has his own special joik by which his friends may recognize him. . ." (19:16). "If anyone breaks the horse in and rides it, I shall give him a rich reward. If, however, he fails it, he will be put in prison" (15:68). Though this sentence begins with a neutral pronoun, "anyone," it soon degenerates to excluding females by using the masculine gender: the presumed sex of anyone who is likely to try to break in a wild horse.

Even in philosophical contexts, people of both sexes become men. Vinoba Bhava bids "All men are brothers. . ." (20:29). "I pray to Him that He should kindle good faith in the heart of every man" (20:33). The dialogue between Yudhisthir and Yaksha in "The Enchanted Pool" typifies the use of "man" to mean "human": " 'What rescues man in danger?' 'Courage is man's salvation in danger. . .' 'Who accompanies a man after death?, 'Dharma'" (36:29-30). A newly born baby is expected to be a "great teacher who will show men how to be. . .good" (20:47).

In her discussion of the "otherness" of women, Simone de Beauvoir (1970:493) shows how men and male achievement have come to represent the standard, the ideal. In comparison, women are always the "other," somehow mysterious, unintelligible and inferior. The language of PITB promotes a similar concept. The best of humanity is masculine. The ideal of the "man" is often used to measure the worth of any person. A character aspires to "meet death like a man" (19:31), implying that to be brave is to be a man, or to be a man means to be brave. Another story incarnates knowledge as a male. All the references to knowledge are in masculine gender. Women not only fare poorly in pronominalization, they are evaluated by comparison with men. When used to describe a woman, "man" is usually intended as a supreme compliment (36:43).

These instances of male-centered language constitute sins of both commission and omission. The responsibility may lie less with the authors than with the way grammar has evolved its patriarchal style. In reference to the human race, it is acceptable to use the words "man" or "men" in Hindi and English. Pronominalization works the same way. Pronouns whose referents could be either female or male automatically become male as in "If anyone doesn't agree, he's mistaken." We are supposed to understand that "he" means "he or she."

But is this really what we understand? Miller and Swift (1976) demonstrate that it is incorrect to presume that "man" is universally understood as a term denoting the image of a "person." The evidence they cite shows that the word "man," and masculine pronouns, almost always bring to mind male human beings. Children find it particularly difficult to discern both women and men in the word "men." Couching all our broad statements about the human race in terms of "man" may have dangerous consequences: female children might not identify with what "man" has done. When "man's" achievements aren't their achievements, they are left as spectators. Referring to a group of women and men as merely "men" implies that men are somehow the legitimate, inside, real members, while women are the exceptions, the outsiders.

What is the effect of sexist language? In *1984*, George Orwell creates a government which controls the population through their language. "Newspeak," the government's new language, contains no words for concepts like freedom. For those who learn "Newspeak," these concepts simply don't exist. Similarly, the male-centered language is hardly consistent with goals of equality between the sexes. In a society where every action or actor is assumed male unless otherwise specified, the concept of the female as a generator of meaningful action may be hampered even before she is born.

Our analysis indicates that the usage of male-centered language in the PITB is rampant, particularly in lessons written in

English by male authors. Authors using sexist, male-centered language write as if catering to a male readership alone. Hypothesis 3 is rejected.

## ANTI-FEMININE STATEMENTS

An anti-feminine statement is a direct condemnation of females as a group. It may be directed against one individual, but its wording, context and tone imply the depreciation of females as a species. We used the incidence of anti-feminine statements as an indicator of the general ideology and/or specific attitudes supporting prejudice against women.

Only 5% of the lessons in our sample (N=19) contained anti-feminine statements. Of these, the number of Hindi (N=10) and English (N=9) lessons was almost equal. Though anti-feminine statements did appear in four lessons authored by females, the majority of such lessons (N=12) were written by males. We did not come across any anti-male statements even mildly comparable to the anti-feminine pronouncements.

The anti-feminine statements found in our sample can be divided into three categories:

1) In a statement that uses her gender as the main basis for her depreciation, a female may be constantly referred to as a silly thing (19:178:79). When not condemned by others, the female actors in the Indian textbooks are shown belittling themselves. "Maggie thought it probable that the small fish would come to her hook and the large ones to Tom's" (19:186). "There I sat, the picture of incompetent womanhood adrift in a masculine world" (16:109), says another woman.

2) In statements which strengthen the notion of female inferiority by asserting the "inherent" superiority of the male, we meet fathers who taunt their sons, "Come on! Are you a girl? It is girls who are stubborn. They are the ones who cry" (12:27). Adults, discussing the ways of this world, complacently agree, "There are certain things in this world that are meant for the males, and higher education is one such thing" (12:216). "The boys' education cannot be treated on a level equal to that of the girls. The males are meant to be educated and achievers. But if the females too start doing the same thing, if they also begin to read English newspapers and discuss politics, then what would

happen to the domestic chores! The he-peacock has feathers, not the she-peacock; the lion has the mane, not the lioness" (12:215). "The male has the beard, not the female" (12:216). A husband considers it beneath himself to discuss "art" with his wife (07:92).

Following the example of such fathers, boys grow up believing that all girls are silly (19:185). These boys want their sisters to be housekeepers only (19:186). To explain their superiority and authority to punish, the boys in the PITB say to girls, ". . .you silly thing. I've got far more money than you, because I'm a boy" (37:22) and "you know I won't hit you, because you are not better than a girl" (37:74). It is no wonder that when these little girls grow up they can only say, "Oh, it's a man's world still" (16:112).

3) The statements that deprecate women as a group condemn the females both in terms of their personal characteristics and social status. Women are put down as fussy do-nothings. "Oh! you women, you make such a fuss over everything" (18:4). Jainendra Kumar Jain, the celebrated Hindi author, would like the young readers to believe that idle gossip preoccupies women. "It is not the nation alone that has politics. The neighborhood has its politics, too. The burden for this kind of politics lies with the women. What-happened-where-and-what-should-have-happened is the kind of gossip that women indulge in" (12:45).

The PITB also portray women as jealous bitch-goddesses who expect the male to devote all his energies toward them. ". . .[The] practice of law is like a jealous woman and a lawyer has to serve her twenty-four hours a day" (34:101), a statement ascribed to Lala Lajpat Rai. Crafty as women are, first they charm men. When the male succumbs to their manipulations, women sponge off his property and live off the fruits of his labor. The male is forever condemned to hard work to provide for them (17:229).

Women are referred to as despicable creatured. Even coach drivers "swear in the name of the horse's grandmother establishing relationships with her. . ." (34:133). They can be called objects without hesitation. Maggie's mother is portrayed growing fond of her tall, dark girl, who is the "only bit of furniture now which she could care for with anxiety and pride" (37:115). They are weak. Christianity is called "a soft religion for women and children, not for men and soldiers" (05:79). They are held res-

ponsible for the worlds' troubles. "Perhaps if women ceased
admiring soldiers in uniforms, wars might end. . ." (37:75).

The PITB present women as vain. "Her hair isn't a woman's
crowning glory. It's the pivot around which her life swings"
(16:110). Educated or not, they must look pretty (12:213, 214).
There is a reiteration of the hackneyed joke that the state should
tax the beauty of females to increase its revenue. Every female
should be allowed to determine the amount of her own assessment. The assumption is that, vain and naive as females are, they
would compete with each other to pay the highest taxes to legitimize their claims to beauty (12:213).

Women are also shown as unworthy of being entrusted with a
secret. "My wife is a woman," a farmer says to himself, "And
women cannot keep secrets. . ." (03:53). They are vulgar (37:63).
They are incompetent weaklings who cannot handle even everyday situations. "In a real emergency, where were women?," asks
a female character (16:109).

And why can't women learn to perform simple chores handl-
ed by ordinary men every day? Why do women continue to be
handicapped by vain pretensions and shallow complacence?
Because "God has made these females cent-percent stupid. I
mean they have no brains at all" (11:132). "What fools these
women are!" (21:24). "I don't know when these females will get
some sense in their heads" (41:116). "Don't you agree that the
females have limited intelligence?" (41:121). "Darwin's principle
of evolution is not applicable to this animal known as the Indian
female. There are no early age, middle-age or modern-age cate-
gorizations applicable to her. She has always belonged to the pre-
historic period. She continues to be in the pre-historic period, and
she would remain for ever in the pre-historic period" (13:15),
declares Dharmvir Bharati.

By including such sexist statements, the Indian textbooks seem
to be in a pre-historic of their own, one in which female education is considered a waste of time, even a danger. The PITB
claim that foolish as women are, they cannot learn anything of
importance. "Girls never learn. . .They are too silly" (37:62).
"Tom had come to the conclusion that no girls could ever construct anything" (37:39). " . . .girls can't do these things, can
they sir?' 'They can pick up a little of everything'. . ." said Mr.
Stelling. . ." 'but they do not go deep into things' " (37:65).

As a result, we are told that the Indian female has no use for formal education. It may only prompt her to ape western mannerisms. She may learn to keep the household accounts in English. But deep down where it counts, she will continue to be what she has always been: irrational, fad-infatuated, ritualistic and superstitious (13:13-30). In educating a female, her parents risk losing their control over her. "I had warned you earlier. If you would have stopped her education at the intermediate level, she would have been under our control" (12:207). Higher education may stigmatize a girl and proportionately diminish her chances for marriage. "I'll be frank with you, sir. We don't need an overly educated girl. Who would cater to her whims? We don't want a *mem-sahib*. At the most a matriculate. . ." (12:215). Since housewives are not supposed to go out and earn livelihoods, they do not need to be educated (12:215). In the ideal family arrangement, the husband is educated but the wife should be just barely literate (12:206, 208). Even if a woman teaches herself to be as good as a man, it is of no use to anybody. "An over clever woman is like a long-tailed sheep—she'll fetch none the bigger price for that" (37:13).

In the Indian textbooks, a daughter is also a no-return liability because only sons can be thought of as old age insurance. The expense of her marriage and dowry often means the depletion of lifetime savings. "Every female, be she a doctor or a sister, is born as a Rs. ten thousand penalty" for her family (11:129). She causes her parents incessant worry and economic hardship. "I am getting sick and tired of those females" (41:106). "These women have me up the creek" (41:123), declare actors one after another.

### Concluding Remarks

A social stigma is a deeply discrediting mark. By definition, a stigmatized person is not quite human, is therefore held to be inferior, and is discriminated against. The stigma of being female may not be comparable to the fate of a person suffering from a serious physical disability, but the anti-feminist strains in the traditional model do move females closer to the status of a despised minority.

It is abvious that the PITB have failed to exclude anti-feminine statements. Hypothesis 4 is rejected.

## FOOTNOTES

[1] In most cases, the number and sex of the  authors/editors was easy
to determine. There were no prefixes before male  names. The textbooks
identified a female either by  mentioning  her  first  name  or giving her
gender a denotative prefix (Miss, Mrs, Sushri, Shrimati).  Where no such
indication was  available  to determine the  sex of an author, and where
only first and middle initials have been provided with  the last name, we
categorized the author as a male. For texts with  a panel of editors,  the
sex  of  the  chief  editor  was  coded  as the sex of the editor. When the
author of a lesson was named "Anonymous,"  or not mentioned  at all
we counted it as an unknown author with indeterminable sex.

CHAPTER VI

# Biography

Protagonists of biographies are effective role models because their traits, personalities, and modes of behavior—considered ideal in a social group—are likely to be projected upon the young.

In our sample, biographies have been analyzed both as lessons and as components of their own subset. When a lesson concentrated on the life, times and activities of a distinguished achiever, we counted that lesson as a biography.[1]

## ACTIVITIES OF THE MALE & FEMALE SUBJECTS OF BIOGRAPHY

MALE SUBJECTS: The 47 male subjects of biography in the PITB appear as rulers, political leaders, social reformers, scholars, artists, authors, soldiers of fortune, scientists, and prophets. Twenty-one (45%) of these are non-Indians.

Among the kings, warriors, and army leaders, Shivaji founds a kingdom by defeating the Mughals. Michael Ruyter rises above his ruffian ways to beccome a famous admiral in the British navy. Among political leaders, Abraham Lincoln, Maharana Pratap, Guru Gobind Singh, and Subhash Bose all wage war for their ideological convictions. Emperor Ashoka, however, realizes the futility of wars and devotes his life to peacemaking. Mahatma Gandhi changes the course of Indian history by adopting non-violence as an instrument for political agitation. Nehru initiates the policy of peaceful non-alignment among the Third World countries. Lal Bahadur Shastri, a poor, fatherless boy, becomes the second prime minister of India. As social reformers, Raja Ram Mohan Roy, Swami Dayanand

Saraswati and Lala Lajpat Rai strive to liberate Hinduism from the stranglehold of orthodoxy. Lokmanya Tilak branches into political journalism to expose the rationale of British rule in India.

In biographies, no Indians appear as adventurers, explorers, or soldiers of fortune like Ambrosio O'Higgins who, though born in a poor Irish hovel, rises to become the viceroy of Peru. Among other foreigners appearing as subjects of biography, Roals Amundsen is the first European to reach the South Pole, Dr. Alain Bombard crosses the Atlantic Ocean alone, and Professor Piccard completes the first successful stratospheric flight.

In the category of scientific personnel, we meet Newton, Pasteur, Edison, Fleming, Nobel, Marconi, Einstein, and Raman. Dr Grenfell builds a civilized community in the wilderness of Newfoundland. Castaret and Haroun Tazieff, both geologists, and Jagdish Chandra Basu, a botanist, risk mortal danger to complete their research. Bhabha develops the atomic potential of India. Hargobind Khorana shares the Nobel Prize for interpreting DNA structures.

Socrates, Jesus, Buddha. Ramakrishna Paramhansa, and Vivekananda appear as prophets, philosophers and great teachers. Charles Dickens and Walter Scott are successful authors and self-made men. Among Indian writers, Bhartendu Harish Chandra, Prem Chand and Nirala give the Hindi literature a proletarian direction. Tagore returns his knighthood to protest against British barbarism. Englishman Dinbandhu Andrews dedicates his life to social work in India. Zakir Hussain, the third president of India, devotes more than 20 years of his youth to the ideals of nationalist education.

*Activities of the female subjects of biography:* In contrast to the 47 male biographies, there are 7 female biographies in the PITB, 3 (43%) of which are about non-Indians.

Helen Keller, deaf and blind from early childhood, learns to read and speak several languages. After finishing college, she champions education for the handicapped. Marie Curie, a dedicated researcher and a successful mother, is the first woman scientist to receive the Nobel Prize. Defying upper-class traditions, Florence Nightingale devotes her life to nursing.

Among political achievers, queen Laxmi Bai raises arms

against the British and dies in action. Sarojini Naidu, a child prodigy and renowned poet, is elected the president of Indian National Congress in 1925 and serves as the governor of U.P. from 1947 to 1949. Kasturba actively participates in the social movements initiated by her husband, M.K. Gandhi. Indira Gandhi is the first female to emerge as Prime Minister in the male-dominant Indian political scene.

## COMPARISON: Male and female subjects of biography

The minor percentage differences between the male and female subjects (Table 13) are not, as they may seem, indicators of parity. The 47 male and 7 female subjects align in 7:1 male-female ratio which is further accentuated by the disparity in the range of their activities and accomplishments. There are no female authors, philosophers, prophets, doctors, adventurers, or explorers as subjects of biography. Only one female appears as a teacher. While one female subject could be coded as a house wife, there are no male subjects of biography devoted to performing domestic, non-marketplace activities.

TABLE 13

### THE BIOGRAPHIC SUBJECTS, OCCUPATION BY SEX

| Occupation | Male | Female |
|---|---|---|
| King/Queen, Warrior, Army Leader | 8% ( 4) | 14% (1) |
| Author, Philosopher, Prophet, Teacher | 28% (13) | 14% (1) |
| Scientist, Doctor, Nurse | 28% (13) | 29% (2) |
| Adventurer, Explorer | 11% ( 5) | 00 (0) |
| Political Leader, Social Reformer | 24% (12) | 29% (2) |
| Housewife | 00 ( 0) | 14% (1) |
| | 100% (47) | 100% (7) |

Since there is no dearth of Indian and foreign females who have distinguished themselves in a variety of endeavors, particularly in the twentieth century, we had hoped that:

H-5. Among the subjects of biography, the PITB will not depict males representing an extremely high proportion of significant achievers.

This has not happened. The editors of the PITB have enhanced the tradition of inequality by maintaining the 7:1 male-female ratio among the subjects of biography. The males continue to dominate as biographic role models. Hypothesis 5 is rejected.

## DIFFERENTIATED SEX ROLE EXPECTATIONS

In the traditional sex role model, a woman's identity was defined predominantly by her familial roles. Marriage, mother-hood and family were considered to be the most crucial compo-nents of a woman's social existence. The PITB sustain this pattern.

A comparison of the frequencies with which various social roles are ascribed to the subjects of biographies affirms the significance of domestic roles in a woman's life (Table 14). Of the total actors, the females were identified as wives and mothers *twice* as often as were males in their comparable roles. Seventy-one percent females appeared in the role of the wife-mother and 86% in the role of the aunt. Among males, 36% were identified as husbands, 32% as fathers and only 4% as uncles. The inter-sexual differences diminished in the per-centages for friend, son/daughter and neighbor roles. As lovers, the males represented a lower percentage (8%) than the females (29%).

TABLE 14

### SOCIAL ROLES ASSIGNED TO THE MALE AND FEMALE SUBJECTS OF BIOGRAPHY

| Roles (Male) | % of total number males (N=47) | Roles (Female) | % of total number females (N=7) |
|---|---|---|---|
| Husband | 36% | Wife | 71% |
| Father | 32% | Mother | 71% |
| Son | 60% | Daughter | 71% |
| Uncle | 4% | Aunt | 86% |
| Friend | 66% | Friend | 57% |
| Lover | 8% | Lover | 29% |
| Neighbor | 6% | Neighbor | 14% |
| Household Head | 36% | Household Head | 14% |

The textbooks almost always categorize the female actors by their marital and parental status. Similarly identification is omitted in the case of a large number of males. The biographies mentioned no divorced males or females, but compared to the 47% of married males, 57% of the females were married. The textbooks seldom failed to mention the marital status of female subjects; however, a substantial number of males were spared such identification. From the information given in the PITB, we could not determine the marital status of half (47%) the males appearing as subjects of biography.

The biographies display an intense eagerness to ensure the identification of a female's parental status, yet the male's parental status receives a casual treatment. While less than one-third (32%) of male biography subjects could be identified as parents, more than two-third (71%) of female subjects could be recognized as such.

In the traditional model of differentiated sex role expectations, girls were seldom specialized to be important marketplace functionaries. Sufficient evidence now indicates that, in industrialized societies, lack of such socialization is likely to instill incompetence and a lack of confidence in girls (Whitehurst, 1977:66—70).

Hoping the PITB would avoid strengthening psychological barriers that sustain inequality between the sexes, we had hypothesized:

H-6. Among the subjects of biography in the PITB, the parental and marital roles of a female shall not be highlighted as more essential to her identity than to the identity of a male.

But in the biographic subset of our sample, the fact of marriage and parenthood is of greater significance for the social placement of female than for the male. Hypothesis 6 is rejected.

## MARKETPLACE AND NON-MARKETPLACE ACTIVITIES

The rationale for the female's exculsion from the Marketplace power structure has been sustained by the notion that a sex-based division of labor is both necessary and functional for society. To determine the extent to which the subjects of the biography help promote or reject the sex-typing of work, we hypothesized that:

H-7. Unlike the traditional, sex role-based segregation of "man's" and "woman's" work, the PITB will depict both the male and female subjects of biography as performing market-place as well as non-marketplace, domestic, activities.

In the following discussion, the non-marketplace domestic activities are defined as activities required to maintain a household, e.g., cooking, house-cleaning, washing clothes, etc.

*Marketplace occupation*

We coded the subjects of biography for the mode by which they acquired marketable skills and their occupations as adults. Our analysis shows a somewhat similar percentage of males (68%) and females (71%) engaged in activities involving the acquisition of marketable skills. Eighty-six percent of the females and 91% of the males were found engaged in market-place occupations outside their homes. An almost equal percentage of males (55%) and females (57%) acquired professional skills through formal instruction. Here again, percentages are meaningless, since the 7:1 numerical discrepancy is upheld. As expected, seven times more males than females learned their occupational skills without any formal education, i.e., through self-taught experimentation.

Accepting the unequivalent ratio, one could argue that, within their own sex group, males and females in marketplace occupations are represented proportionally. This raises a point crucial to any discussion involving biography subjects. For the most part, biographies are written about individuals who have made significant contributions through high prestige, market-place occupations. Their notoriety or renown for their uniqueness. Since female achievers are not likely to be timorous toadies, we would not expect authors to confine them to feminine stereotypes. Rather, we would expect their scores for occupations and personality traits to be similar to the scores of male achievers. Without the corresponding achievement-traits their accomplishments would appear ridiculously incongruous.

Unfortunately, some PITB authors, victims of patriarchal deception, seem to be hesitant about accepting this. They are quick to qualify a female's achievement by subserviating it to the masculine principle. A female in their writings is noteworthy not by the virtue of her achievements, but because she acts like a man. "Though a woman," writes G.R. Swami referring to Sarojini Naidu, "she played a part that any man might be proud of" (36:44).

## Non-marketplace activities

The feminist perspective defines the sex role-based non-marketplace service work as being routinely helpful with servitudinal tones and little economic recognition, as compared to more rewarding marketplace occupations.

To verify H-7, we examined the content of biographies for the circumstances under which males and females were shown performing non-marketplace work. We found that not only was there a greater percentage of females (female—29%, male—19%) depicted as performing non-marketplace activities, but the purpose of these activities also differed for the two sexes.

The females seem to be performing the non-marketplace activities as an integral part of their social roles. Kasturba cooks, cleans and does heavier household chores as Mahatma Gandhi's wife. Marie Curie, a full-time research scientist, keeps house and raises children.

The males even when acting out their primary-group roles, tend to perform non-marketplace activities more as exception than the rule. While in exile, Maharana Pratap cooks meal for his children. Tagore takes care of his wife's personal needs. Nirala cooks for his friends. But none of the males performs non-marketplace chores because he is bound by sex role expectations similar to those applicable to females. Tagore looks after his wife's personal needs only when she is on her death bed. Nirala cooks because he likes to use his culinary skills to please his friends. Maharana Pratap, Professor Piccard and Dr. Bombard cook because the alternative is death by starvation. Nowhere else in the biographies are these actors shown routinely performing non-marketplace chores.

In some cases, the males undertake non-marketplace chores as messianic underprops to bolster their occupational goals. Every Tuesday, Grenfell cleans the house of old Williams, a patient who has no legs. When King George's messenger arrives with the news of knighthood awarded to Grenfell, the dedicated doctor is on his knees, scrubbing the floor. Jesus is credited with similar efforts to care for the sick. Mahatma Gandhi's emphasis on male, as well as female, engagement in non-marketplace activities comes from his ideological objective of dignifying the tasks associated with untouchables and the overall ideal of human equality. He insists[5] that the residents of his *ashram* and his other companions clean their own latrines and perform other chores on a rotating basis.

These, however, are idealistic gestures and are presented as such. For everyday living, the performance of non-marketplace activities by subjects of biographies conveys a different message: When females perform non-marketplace activities, they do them as a "natural" and "necessary" extension of their domesticated social selves. When males perform non-marketplace activities, they do them as a supplement which is definitely not as "natural" or "necessary" to their occupational roles. Thus, the men receive praise for performing tasks which women are expected to do habitually, without remuneration.

To wit, what is sauce for the goose is poison for the gander. Owing to the comparative insignificance of non-marketplace, domestic activities in the lives of the male subjects of biography, Hypothesis 7 is rejected.

## INDIVIDUAL CHARACTERISTICS

We also tried to examine the extent to which traditional stereo-types were replicated in the personality traits ascribed to the subjects of biography. Each subject was scored on a list of pair-ed characteristics (Table 15). The percentages reported for every characteristic signify the percentage of characters in each sex group who exhibited that particular quality. For example, "Independent—98%" means that on the basis of evidence avail-able from the content of biographies, 98% of the male subjects could be coded as "Independent."

Most male and female subjects of biography appeared on the positive end of the following pairings: Task-oriented: Confused, Assertive: Non-assertive, Leader: Follower, Clever: Incompetent, Strong (Character): Weak (Character), Brave: Fearful.

Yet even the characterization of significant achievers did not escape sex role bias. In Table 15, male actors appeared as more generous than the females. In the Selfish: Selfless pairing of

TABLE 15

## INDIVIDUAL CHARACTERISTICS ASSIGNED TO THE SUBJECTS OF THE BIOGRAPHIES, BY SEX

| | MALE | | FEMALE | |
| | percentage | number | percentage | number |
| --- | --- | --- | --- | --- |
| Independent | 98 | 46 | 71 | 5 |
| Dependent | 2 | 1 | 14 | 1 |
| Indeterminable | 0 | | 14 | 1 |
| Selfish | 70 | 33 | 43 | 3 |
| Selfless | 0 | | 28 | 2 |
| Indeterminable | 30 | 14 | 28 | 2 |
| Task-oriented | 100 | 47 | 86 | 6 |
| Confused | 0 | | 14 | 1 |
| Indeterminable | 0 | | 0 | |
| Assertive | 83 | 39 | 71 | 5 |
| Non-assertive | 2 | 1 | 14 | 1 |
| Indeterminable | 15 | 7 | 15 | 1 |
| Innovative | 94 | 44 | 57 | 4 |
| Imitative | 0 | | 14 | 1 |
| Indeterminable | 6 | 3 | 28 | 2 |
| Leader | 87 | 41 | 86 | 6 |
| Follower | 0 | | 14 | 1 |
| Indeterminable | 13 | 3 | 0 | |
| Clever | 62 | 29 | 71 | 5 |
| Incompetent | 0 | | 14 | 1 |
| Indeterminable | 38 | 18 | 14 | 1 |
| Strong (Physical) | 66 | 31 | 86 | 6 |
| Fragile | 4 | 2 | 0 | |
| Indeterminable | 30 | 14 | 14 | 1 |
| Strong (Character) | 81 | 38 | 86 | 6 |
| Weak | 0 | | 0 | |
| Indeterminable | 19 | 9 | 14 | 1 |
| Brave | 77 | 36 | 71 | 5 |
| Fearful | 0 | | 0 | |
| Indeterminable | 23 | 11 | 29 | 2 |
| Generous | 60 | 28 | 29 | 2 |
| Petty | 2 | 1 | 0 | |
| Indeterminable | 38 | 18 | 71 | 5 |

characteristics, women emerged less selfish and more selfless than men.

Summarizing the data on childhood experiences and achievement, Hoffman (1972) concluded that girls have higher affiliative

needs, and their achievement behavior is motivated by a desire
to please. If their achievement behavior comes into conflict with
affiliation, achievement is likely to be sacrificed. In our data, the
percentage difference in a Innovative: Imitative category adhered
to Hoffman's stereotype. As compared to 94% of the males, only
57% of the females subjects of biography appeared as innovative.

An equally significant male-female difference appeared in the
assignment of "Independent" as a characteristic in the Independent: Dependent pairing. While 98% of the subjects could be
coded as independent, only 71% of the females qualified for
inclusion in the same category.

Earlier we observed the comparatively greater significance
assigned to the primary group roles in the life of females. An
explanation for the differences shown here is rooted in the same
ground. The *differentiated* preponderance of non-marketplace
roles offers the male a wide choice of secondary and non-family
groups with which to associate. The familiy groups continue to be
more significant in the female's life. If these groups are the basic
and most crucial arena for social interaction, women are likely
to learn not to disrupt their primary group life by independent
behavior.

## FOOTNOTES

[1]In assigning characteristics to the subjects of biographies, we used
the content of lessons as our *only* source of information. For example,
the marital status of various actors is well known. But if such status was
indeterminable from the content of the biographical sketch, we disregarded the fact known outside the world of textbooks and coded this status as
indeterminable.

We found a total of 71 lessons that could have been counted as biographies. In L-192 and L-207, there was very little information on the
main character. L-838 focused on the activities of a single individual
catching sharks by hand. But other than referring to the main character
by his first name, the lesson provided greater detail on the activities of
the sharks than on those of human beings. To avoid duplication, thirteen
more lessons (Lesson identification numbers: 103, 120, 188, 199, 213, 215,
216, 219, 281, 310, 323, 324, 335) were excluded from the final list that
includes 54 biographies.

# CHAPTER VII

# Leading Actors and Authority Relationships

Continuing the line of inquiry pursued in the last chapter, we shall now examine the male-female ratio of leading actors in our *total* sample of 353 lessons. To determine the extent of departure from male dominance in group action and in individual creativity, we shall also report our findings on male-female authority relationships.

## SEX RATIO OF HUMAN CHARACTERS IN THE PITB

In our sub-sample of biographic materials, males represented an extremely high proportion of significant achievers. To see if a similar dominance of male characters occurs in the total sample, we hypothesize:

H-8. The males will not constitute a heavy majority of leading characters in the PITB.

To generate evidence for testing H-8, we coded the sex ratio of total 1) human characters and 2) leading characters in the PITB.[1] We counted a total of 3,798 human characters. Eighty-one per cent of these were males, 19% were females.

### Sex of the Leading Characters

We also counted the sex of persons who played the most important part, or received considerably more attention than other actors in the plot of a lesson. Males emerged as leading characters in 75% of the lesson. In 17% of the lessons, both males *and* females emerged as leading characters. Only in 8% of the lessons could the females be characterized as the sole leading character.

The dominance of males as leading characters decreased only

in lessons written by females. In these, 39% of the leading characters were women. However, 36% of the lessons authored by women still cast males in the lead. Thus, while the probability of females leads increased in lessons written by other females, this increase was, comparatively, so slight that it was insignificant.

Only 4% (N=10) of the lessons witten by male authors and females as the leading characters. Seventy-five per cent of the lessons written by anonymous authors and *all* the lessons written by males *and* females had male leading characters. Differences in language, type of lesson, probable origin and source did not affect the preponderance of males as leading characters.

In view of the above, Hypothesis 8 is rejected.

## DECISION-MAKING

To study sex role modeling and the decision-making processes in our sample, we looked at situations that included decision-making by male and female characters. To understand the modes of gender-based dominance, we examined both the issues and mechanics of decision-making. For coding purposes, a decision-making situation was defined as a situation in which the male(s) and female(s) interact to arrive at a decision. The actor who achieved his/her intended goal(s) was coded as the dominant actor. One out of five lessons in our sample contained decision-making situations (N=71).

The females slightly dominate the number of total decision-making situations (49% compared to 43% for males). Males and females made joint decisions in only 9% of the total decision-making situations.[2]

The following evidence on decision-making is discussed under three categories: 1) Joint decision-making, 2) Male-dominant decision-making, 3) Female-dominant decision-making.

### Evidence for Male and Female Joint Dominance

In this category, the decision-making process does not always resolve issues in favor of either sex. In many cases, sex role related dominance is altogether absent. Love, not dominance, motivates Jim and Della when each one gives up his/her most valuable possession to please the other (L-151). Loyalty to the ruler is the overriding factor in a couple's decision to sacrifice their son to save their kingdom (L-034). Such decisions, where neither sex clearly dominates, also relate to husband-wife separation, joining the political protest against parents' wishes, and finding the right medicinal treatment for a sick quest.

## Evidence for Male-Dominant Decision-Making

In instances of male-dominant, *marketplace* decision-making, the issues range from creating a unique human being to fleecing a generous king. An inventor decides to continue his research despite the hostility of his superstitious neighbors (L-158). A king surrenders his kingdom in the face of defeat by a powerful enemy (L-009). To prepare for his civil service tests, a candidate moves to another locale where he can study without interruptions from his temperamental wife who demands his attention (L-028).

Males dominant the *non-marketplace* decision-making in the following areas: husband's right to give away the wife's property, reactions to a female's advice in family matters, role of parents in their children's lives, control of the female's obedience or compliance by command alone, treatment of the wanted and unwanted quests, household budgeting, adoption and marital arrangements.

## Evidence for Female Dominant Decision-Making

The *marketplace* decisions made by women as royalty are generally free of interference by males. Jija Bai, Karmavati and Laxmibai receive complete obedience from their male generals. Lady Macbeth operates in an environment free of any constraints by her husband (L-289). Portia is unhampered by the pugnacity of her adversaries. Among the commoners, Panna Dhaai, the maidservant entrusted with the life of the heir-prince, carries out her obligation at the cost of her own son's life (L-265). Madhoolika, when asked for her choice of reward for saving the kingdom of Koshal, asks to be judged along with her lover Arun, a condemned prisoner (L-266). Florence Nightingale overrides the bigoted military officers who resent a female telling them how to run the health care system for wounded soldiers (L-199).

In *non-marketplace* situations, females are most apt to take control when the issue at hand fundamentally concerns their own lives. The number of plots hinging on the choice of a husband indicates the importance of such decisions. Various females assert themselves in the choice of their spouses (L-225, L-228, L-229, L-295). Many female-dominant situations involve the females' role in the lives of their children, a context in which the females' role dominance is sometimes augmented by the prerogatives of age and guardianship (L-134). Other *non-marketplace* issues which females dominate relate to the treatment of guests, responsibility for children, accompanying a husband to his workplace, acceptance of arranged marriage, behavior in stress situations, household budgeting, and moral guidance.

## Males and Females in Decision-Making Situations: A comparison

Ideally, the traditional sex role model expected the male to dominate in decision-making. However, the marketplace hierarchy made it impossible for every male to be on top of every situation. Hence, the acquired urge to dominate expressed itself most frequently in the home. Males incurred the admiration of others for being masters of their own households.

Recent studies of the relationship between play activity and socialization indicate how, through childhood and adolescent games, most boys receive achievement training while girls receive more obedience and responsibility (Stoll, 1974:80 ff). Hoping the textbooks of India would not reinforce the traditional modes of sexist decision-making, we had hypothesized:

H-9. In decision making situations involving the sexes, the PITB will not depict the male as more likely to dominate the decision-making process, nor will his right to dominate be derived from his sex role prerogatives rather than from his problem-solving competency.

As reported in the beginning of this section, our frequency count shows a statistical parity between the males and females. The females even appear to have a slightly better chance of dominating decision-making. But once we examine the *mechanics of dominance*, we find that the probability of female dominance in decision-making processes is heavily qualified by subtle yet effective patriarchal constraints. Our evidence clearly illustrates how traditional sex role expectations jeopardize the apparent equality in decision-making in the PITB.

Take first, the plots with male dominant decision-making situations. Given the nature of cases in this category, the males lead in most of the situations. But more interesting are the implications inherent in the mechanics of male dominance. More than once, these plots imply a subtle degradation of the female's personality and her social roles. It is not enough that the male leads. Perhaps to ensure male ascendancy, the female's capabilities are repeatedly discountenanced. This is particularly true when the decisions involve a husband and wife. After Nala loses his kingdom by gambling, he never asks his wife what she would like to do. He simply deserts her in the forest (L-008). In the case of Wong Shin Ching, the candidate studying for his civil service examination, his young wife appears as the source of trouble. That Ching disregards his wife's whims is understandable. But male characters like Mr. Tulliver seldom deem it proper even to seek their wives' opinion. Another fleeing king never explains the rationale of his acts to his wife; he just abandons the kingdom. As expected, she follows (L-009).

Males as husbands are presented as more able judges in even simple decisions. This theme is developed to ridiculous extremes. As David Copperfield arrives on his aunt's doorstep, the aunt, who is otherwise sensible, sturdy, and dominant in her relationships with other people, turns to her somewhat loony husband for advice on how to treat the boy. When a woman with a strong character seeks the opinion of a half-crazy male, the implication is clear. A male, even a mentally unstable one, is expected to take control in every crisis. Any independence a woman may demonstrate supposedly crumbles at the slightest pressure (L-137). Maggie's fits of self-assertion are presented as superficial and childish. She denies Tom's power over her life when he objects to her relationship with Philip. But, in fact, she never does see Philip again, and the relationship ends perhaps as a tribute to Tom's dominance (L-327). Even the children in the plots of PITB presuppose the female's dependence on male guidance (L-140).

In joint decision-making, the deprecation of the female continues unabated. The stereotype of the female as a creature of spiteful whim is authenticated when a husband and wife argue about the type of treatment, Western or Ayurvedic-cum-witchcraft, to be administered to a patient. The issue remains unresolved, but the debate is likely to convince the readers that the reasoning and tastes of the female are, as the husband charges, irrational, archaic and foolish. By her demeanor during the argument, she is portrayed as a well-meaning, but fatuous housewife (L-353).

In most instances, a woman's dominance in non-marketplace issues is rooted in her responsibilities as a housewife. The tasks of hospitality, for example, is one area where she can often dominate. But even here, her dominance is subject to the degree of cooperation she receives from her husband. This is true even when the decisions involve chores performed exclusively by the female, such as cooking for guests (L-048, L-062, L-264, L-299). The female may seem to dominate a decision, when actually it is convenient for the male to give her enough rope to hang herself. The freedom enjoyed by Jill only proves her incompetence in financial matters (L-332). When another housewife decides to adopt a street urchin, her husband humors her. As the plot unfolds, it becomes clear that he is giving her this freedom only to prove his low estimate of her perspicacity (L-066). A woman who is all talk and not capable of handling even a street urchln, the readers may conclude, is better off not making a fool of herself by competing with adult males. This lesson also underlines how male indifference to child-rearing gives responsibility by default to females in the household. Women, the reader will conclude, are delegated the responsibility for child rearing because men cannot be bothered.

The woman as custodian of morality is another recurrent image which provides females with limited authority in some decision-making situations. A wife prevents her husband from publishing pornography just to make money (L-260). The question of female dominance here assumes a subtler tone than in the cases of women who seek to control their own marital status. Here the female tries to persuade her husband to change his decision, but since he remains the ultimate actor, this plot subliminally confirms that a woman's only route to power is through subtle manipulation of the male ego.

When not wanting to play the subaltern accessory, a female

may coquettishly provoke the male into a non-routine activity to relieve her own boredom. Confided in a long enduring system of patriarchic authority, women learn to manipulate men to supply their every need. Inspiration is a traditional euphemism for such manipulation. The female companion to the Creator of the Universe challenges the male for her own entertainment. He accepts the challenge. What is interesting is not his dominance but the complacence with which the dependence of women is vaingloriously accepted, even welcomed in such situations (L-352).

Women who deny their traditional roles and attempt to make decisions are portrayed as being more perverse or vulgar than women who passively accept male dominance. Prince Lakshman graphically demonstrates this theme as he cuts off the nose and ears of the Demon Princess Shurpanakha because she proposes to him. By his act of mutilation, Lakshman renders her not only grotesque, but also ineffective to ever again approach a man so boldly (L-235).

Difficulties for "misfit" women still focus mainly on domestic relationships, and males are given ultimate authority for resolving problems (L-140). A father keenly interested in marrying off his daughter presents her to prospective in-laws as a semi-literate doll, although she is actually an educated, self-respecting individual (L-115). Another plot implies that educated women do not deserve more respect than their uneducated but docile counterparts. If anything, educated women are more troublesome and require more supervision.

Usually the female's lifestyle, whether she is educated or not, is designed for the convenience of a man. King Dushyant insists that Shakuntala marry him immediately so that he can attend to important affairs of state. Although the bride wants to wait for her godfather, Kanva, to return and perform a more appropriate ceremony, the plot does not admit the possibility that Shakuntala should ask the king to come back after Kanva arrives (L-033). In rare instances when a woman decides to show her social dominance, she acts so that she can be near a man to offer emotional and ideological support. Savitri persuades Satyavan to let her accompany him to his workplace because, unbeknown to him, he is due to die on that day (L-035). The males in the PITB are seldom subjected to similar supportive obligations.

In contests where the females emerge as dominant decision-makers, their very uniqueness undermines the positive impact of their victories. In many ways, both Savitri and Miss Holmes have little in common with an average girl. Deviating from the post-Vedic traditional stereotype, Savitri not only chooses her own husband, she also sticks to her decision against her parent's wishes. Miss Holmes is a British girl, and British girls in general are comparatively free of the restraints imposed on Indian girls. An Indian reader may admire Miss Holmes for independence, but may not necessarily be able to identify with the role model she presents.

Similarly, Sarojini Naidu's decision to marry out of her caste is not as great a social risk as it may initially appear. Her parents are well-educated professionals. The man she chooses to marry is a physician. A child prodigy, she has been educated in England during the earlier quarter of this century when most Indian women did not even go to their hometown schools. But how many other women in the PITB can stand behind a similar protective shield of exceptional achievement ? Very few. When even a princess is banished from the place for choosing her own husband, the average female can seldom hope to defy the male-oriented traditions without inviting heavy penalties. A woman who marries outside her caste or a young widow who chooses not to remarry is either shunned or condemned outright in the PITB. When a young widow scorns the lecherous advances of local romeos and insists on earning an independent living, the villagers think she is insolent and ostracize her (L-307). Such treatment of the unattached, adult female labels her as either an aberration or a threat to the male-centered belief system. In Indian textbooks, a woman is considered incomplete if she is not dependent on a male.

In the story "Mamta", the Hindu Princess Mamta refuses to accept the man her father has chosen for her. However, the assertion of her individuality is not inspired by what one generally understands as individualism. She uses the traditional Hinduist disapproval and distrust of Muslims as the rationale for her rejection (L-094). One is tempted to ask: would she have rejected him if he had been ugly and salacious, but a Hindu prince ? Mamta's choice of religious grounds as her basis for rejecting an arranged marriage heavily qualifies the element of independence implicit in such a decision. A female is obligated to provide an ideological justification for her decision to remain single. She must have an excuse. She cannot choose to be single because it is her preference.

## Concluding Remarks

In view of the above, the statistical evidence for male-female parity of dominance in decision-making seems misleading. The frequency count does provide the female with some equality. But the traditional stance of male dominance is kept intact in the PITB model. Often, the male's right to dominate a decision is derived from his sex role prerogatives. Hypothesis 9 is rejected.

## AUTHORITY RELATIONSHIPS

### Methodology

To determine male-female differences in the extent of authority and dominance ascribed to the actors in our sample, we coded our main characters on a two-dimensional, three-point scale of dominance-subservience. The plots were examined to see if an actor could be categorized as: 1) Dominant, 2) Cooperative, 3) Subservient. Categories 1 and 3 were treated as mutually exclusive. To collapse categories, however, the dominant only, cooperative only, and subservient only categories were combined to produce a two-dimensional distribution. Thus, an individual could be coded in more than one category, as either dominant-cooperative or cooperative subservient. The frequency was combined to get the percentages for the dominant dimension. The frequencies for cooperative only, subservient only, and cooperative subservient main characters were put together in a single category to get the percentages for the subservient dimension. Table 16 shows this two-dimensional distribution. The level of significance for Table 16 is high.

To tabulate the results reported in Table 16, we coded a total of 571 main characters (79% male, 21% female). Seventy-five percent of all main characters were composed of dominant males, while dominant females represented only 16% of the total.

TABLE 16

AUTHORITY RELATIONSHIPS, MAIN CHARACTER BY SEX

|  | *Male* | *Female* |
|---|---|---|
| Dominant | 94% | 76% |
|  | (425) | (90) |
| Subservient | 6% | 24% |
|  | (27) | (29) |
|  | 100% | 100% |
|  | (452) | (119) |

Chi-square = 36
df = 1
Level of Significance = .001

Whe taken separately, however, 76% (N=91) of the female main characters appeared to be "dominant". This unexpected disproportion can be ascribed to the definition of a main character. Generally, a main character is active and at the center of events. Still, even this higher than expected percentage of dominant female main characters pales against the hefty 94% (N=427) of dominant males. Also, only 6% of male main characters could be classified as "subservient," compared to 24% of the females in this group.

To further verify, we also examined the authority relationships in the subset of biographies. The biographies were read to determine if an actor's relationship with other actors could be termed as (1) dominant, (2) cooperative, or (3) subservient. Again categories 1 and 3 were treated as mutually exclusive.

In Table 14, the percentage of males appearing as heads of a household (36%) was more than twice as high as the percentage for the females appearing as the heads of households (14%). But the other data in the biographic subset *do not* confirm the overall bias in favor of the males. The percentage of the male actors (94%) who have a dominant and/or cooperative relationship with other actors is not significantly different from the percentage of female actors (86%) enjoying similar relationships.

We cannot assume that these figures signal a weakness in the otherwise armor-plated male dominance evident in the total sample. Female subjects of biography dominate as an accompaniment to their outstanding personal achievements. It would be naive to suggest that their dominance is a consequence of sex role equality in the PITB. Nothing seems to affect the preponderance of males who represent an overwhelming majority of dominant actors in the total sample of main characters.

To determine the male-female differences in the extent of authority and dominance ascribed to the actors in our sample, we had hypothesized:

H—10. The PITB will not depict the male as more likely to be dominant-cooperative in social and marketplace authority relationships, while depicting the female as more likely to be cooperative-subservient.

Since the males in the PITB are shown more likely to be dominant-cooperative while the females are depicted as more likely to be cooperative-subservient, Hypothesis 10 is rejected.

## SEX ROLE VICTIMIZATION

We studied the incidence of sex role victimization as an indicator of authority relationships. We understand sex role victimization to be the persecution of an individual because of role restrictions inherent in his/her gender based social placement.

Six percent (N=21) of the total lessons in our sample contained instances of sex role victimization. We found only one instance where a male could be coded as a sex role victim. There are more instances of sex role victimization in Hindi lessons (Hindi—57%, English—43%). Overall, regardless of the sex of the author, kind of lesson, probable origins, or source of the plot, *the females constitute an overwhelming majority (95%, (N=120) of the sex role victims* in both Hindi and English language lessons. In only three instances did the female act as the victimizer. All these instances, and one instance of the male and female acting together as victimizers, were fouud in Hindi language lessons.

The male also emerged as the instrument of victimization in stories and plays of both Indian and non-Indian origins. A combination of verbal and physical aggression was the most prominent mode of victimization.

### Female as a Victimizer

In the single instance where a female victimizes a male, the finicky wife of a retired police officer tries to run her husband's life according to her erratic and orthodox religious regimen. Using her leverage as the housewife, she spends a substantial part of his pension on the ritualistic feeding of animals and religious ceremonies, leaving little for the upkeep of the house. The male is depicted perpetually broke, destitute and starved (L—116).

In other cases, females act as agents of victimization against other females. An aunt beats up the young girl she wants to displace from the palace (L—228). An orthodox mother-in-law ostracizes her son for marrying out of caste (L—313). A similar but more derisive form of social ostracism is practiced by villagers, the females in particular, who start a whisper campaign to malign a low-caste but self-respecting widow (L—307).

### Male as a Victimizer

With the exception of one case cited above (L—116), the female is the victim in all instances of sex role victimization. The victimizers use physical aggression, verbal aggression or a combination of the two.

While using *verbal* aggression, the male can resort to vicious rumor campaigns, decision, or downright abuse. In his use of *physical* aggression, the Ideal Male binds the female's feet with chains to put her in her place (L—065). A beautiful woman is badly disfigured when she and her husband are involved in a railway accident (L—061). The husband, infatuated with his wife's former beauty, cannot endure the reality of her imperfection. He kills her. Although the author tries to elevate such violence as an ultimate tribute to beauty, the fact remains that the husband never stops to consider that his wife might prefer to live, however disfigured she may be. The assumption, of course, is that without her beauty, a woman's entire existence is superfluous. Any imperfection lessens her value like depreciation on a damaged figurine. By romanticizing the murder as a crime of passion, the lesson strengthens the romantic play of extremist, inhuman reactions. Though the lover is punished by death for the murder, the play condones his violence. One wonders if Lady Chatterley would have received approval in the PITB had she murdered her husband after he became paralyzed from an accident.

When married and living with her husband, a wife may still get the shorter end of the deal. The husband may make her pay for financial misadventures he undertook without consulting. her. Mr. Tulliver constantly engages in legal disputes without ever consulting Mrs. Tulliver or listening to her advice. In the end, he loses all, including the precious possessions Mrs. Tulliver owned before marriage (L—327).

In the combined use of physical and verbal aggression, the males boldly display all their fangs and claws. An alcoholic contemptuously berates his wife's loyalty to him, taunts her for being virtuous, abuses her, beats her and snatches away her hard-earned money to support his drinking bouts (L—344). When one village woman refuses to cater to the sexual whims of her sick husband's brothers, they beat her up, throw her in a ditch and leave her for dead (L—262). But the poor and ignorant do not have a monopoly on victimization. An educated, successful businessman feels no qualms about abusing his wife (L—113). A magician beats a princess when she refuses to marry him (L—229).

What surprises us most is not the cruelty or vulgarity of these acts, but the insensitivity with which males go about committing their indiscretions, violations, desertions and kidnappings. A farmer sweet talks his aging aunt into turning her property over to him. After the transfer is completed, he denies her even the basic amenities of life (L—032). To fulfill the ideal of male friendship, a bridegroom leaves his bride at the altar in the middle of the ceremony. Ignoring the protests of his kith and kin, he goes into the battlefield where he is killed. At no time is there any inkling of consideration for the girl who has been condemned to widowhood by his feudal code of ethics (L—126).

The inclusion of Kasturba as a subject of biography well illustrates the ideological bias in the male-female authority relationship in the PITB. The title of this biographical piece reads, "Kasturbai—An Ideal Wife." Kasturba is presented as a woman dominated by her husband, M.K. Gandhi—a man who tyrannically expects his wife to live by a script he has written without her consultation. He has the ultimate say in all matters. "Like most of the Hindu wives of her time, she believed that what her husband did was right" (L—214). He rebukes her in front of everybody, berating her like a child for some minor omission. She mildly protests or cries, but eventually she acquiesces. Hers is not to reason why. So strong is her commitment to the creed of wifely service, that she actually minds when not called upon to perform the routine chores of hospitality ascribed to the common Indian wife.

Eventually, believing in the political causes of her husband, she takes part in the popular agitation, gets arrested and, to the surprise of our female biographer, she "even made some speeches" (L—214). This is reminiscent of Shaw's skepticism about a politically conscious woman whom he compared to a dog walking on its hind legs and talking in English. But Kusturba's political involvement is due to her loyalty rather than any ideological enlightenment. "She took part in the political struggle as a mark of loyalty and devotion to her husband" (L—214). In Kasturba, we have a woman totally dominated by her husband. She is ideally self-sacrificing to the point of being a non-individual, silent and completely devoted to the ideals chosen by her husband. An ideal Indian wife indeed!

To determine sex role-based differences in the social power exercised by the two sexes in the traditional and the PITB model, we had hypothesized:

H—11. The females in the PITB will not be victimized to a greater extent than the males, through evaluative degradation, role restraint and actual physical violation.

Our analysis shows that not only do the PITB present females as victims and males as victimizers, the PITB also seem to condone the victimization of the female by promoting an inequalitarian model of sex role relationships. Hypothesis 11 is rejected.

## FOOTNOTES

[1]To determine the number of human characters in a lesson, we counted the characters that (1) were actually involved in the plot and/or (2) were referred to in a lesson. The final count for a lesson combined the number of actual actors and the references to persons with determinable sex. The only exception to this method of counting was in lessons where the author referred to groups or people in numbers, e.g., thousands of soldiers. Such enumeration was excluded from our tally. In "A Voyage to Lilliput," for example, the author mentions large

numbers of carpenters, engineers and other workers, totalling more than a thousand males. In such instances, we counted only the major actors and treated the large (numbered by the author) teams of workers as an undefined mass. Most such groups—armies, teams, populations—are generally not enumerated by authors in other lessons.

[2]No significant differences in the incidence of male-female dominance could be found in categories of authors's sex, kind of lesson and the lessons of non-Indian origin. The females, however, appear dominant in Hindi language lessons and lessons of Indian origin. In Hindi language lessons, females dominate 70% of the decision-making situations, while they appear dominant in 42% of the English language lessons. In our analysis of favorable images and anti-feminine statements, we had found no significant differences in the language category. Hence the emergence of the female as a dominant actor in Hindi lessons is significant.

# CHAPTER VIII

# Occupational Role Models

India's occupational structure is a curious mixture of tradition and modernity. While the country can boast of Nobel Prize-winners, most Indians work in labor-intensive industries which offer meagre occupational mobility. Industrialization, however, is already promoting the technical and professional occupations which are more characteristic of modern than traditional India. These occupations require skill levels, command higher incomes, and offer greater autonomy and a better chance of upward mobility.

The following three processes appear dominant in this context: 1) increasing specialization, 2) total upgrading of skill requirements, and 3) rising aspirations for greater movement both within and between the existing and evolving occupational stratas (Moore, 1965). To facilitate these processes, the educational and occupational systems of India must harmonize: each must supply what the other needs.

In considering the content of school textbooks important to socialization for adult career aspirations, we do not deny the role of other variables that affect the realization of such aspirations. Variations in individual aptitudes and competence, individual SES, and economic conditions governing employment clearly affect entry into the job market. But these do not minimize the importance of formal schooling in the development of occupational aspirations. As Indian society progresses from an ascriptive to an achievement-orientation, formal education will help its young internalize the new norms of success. Occupational role models will increasingly determine the motivation to succeed in the competitive marketplace.

Further, as in other societies on the path of industrialization,

young people in India are likely to suffer from a crisis of identification in occupational role modeling. Because the world of
adults and children was contiguous in pre-industrial societies, the
young could acquire their occupational role models with relative
ease. Daughters watching their mothers at work may have a
similar opportunity in industrial societies, but even this opportunity lends itself only to acquiring non-marketplace skills. The
boys and girls of present-day India, as in other technological
societies, are generally excluded from any direct involvement in
their parent's professions. Given this separation, the occupational role models presented in the textbooks are likely to have a
significant impact on occupational socialization.

We have understood an occupation to be ". . . a social construct and its performance, a social role or a set of roles" (Moore,
1969: 868), Thus, an occupation requires task-oriented expertise
as well as behavioral norms necessary for the successful appli-
cation of this expertise. Any difference of socialization in the preferred role models will accordingly influence the choice and
motivation for occupational achievement.

To determine the nature of occupational role modeling in the
post-independence textbooks (PITB), we hypothesize:

H-12. As compared to the traditionally sexist division of
labor, the range and diversity of occupations in the PITB will be
similar for males and females.

To test Hypothesis 12, we have examined the occupations
assigned to the male and female characters in the PITB from
three perspectives: 1) the industrial and non-industrial orientation of occupations, 2) range and diversity of occupations, and
3) occupational prestige scores.

## Methodology for Counting Occupations in the PITB

In coding the incidence of an occupation, our main purpose
was to determine the range and diversity of occupations assigned
to male and female characters in the PITB model. This being the
case, we limited the frequency count of an occupation in a lesson
to one incidence, regardless of the number of characters belong-
ing to that occupation. For example, if there were six farmers,
two kings, one soldier and four housewives in one lesson, each
occupation was entered only once in the frequency count for that
particular lesson. The cumulative frequency of an occupation

determined its frequency score (e.g,, King (87) signifies that the occupation of king appeared in 87 lessons; 87 is its frequency score.

## INDUSTRIAL AND NON-INDUSTRIAL ORIENTATION OF OCCUPATIONS IN THE PITB

We wanted to see if the PITB model sustains or rejects the traditional orientation vis-a-vis an orientation conducive to the needs of an industrialized society. To this end, we divided the male and female occupations in the PITB into three categories: 1) occupations more likely to be found in traditional societies, 2) occupations more likely to be found in industrial societies, and 3) occupations common to both traditional and industrial societies. The terms "traditional" and "industrial" are used here as ideal types in the evolution of a society from the lower to the higher stages of industrialization. The lists of male and female occupations, grouped by society type, are given in Appendix E.

A look at the list of total occupations assigned to the female characters (Appendix E) indicate that the PITB do assign females some occupations ($N=12$, 2% of the total) that were not normally available to them in the traditional model. These are: violin teacher, dietician, doctor—medical, minister—political, pathologist, priest, prime minister, professor, scientist, social worker, and teacher of the deaf. But in Table 17, most female occupations are concentrated in the category of occpations likely to be found in traditional societies. In the row totals, 44% of the female-filled occupations, as compared to 27% of the male occupations, fall in the traditional category. When we use the distribution of occupations likely to be found in industrial societies, the female scores even more poorly. Twenty-four percent of the male occupations fall in the category of occupations most likely to be found in industrialized societies, while the female's share for this category is 17%.

Any significant detraditionalization of Indian occupational structures would involve more than a token entry of females in non-traditional, marketplace occupations. It would require an unequivocal rejection of the assumptions underlying the traditional model. Only then can India's occupational profile be restructured to adhere to the ideal of non-sexist interchangeability

TABLE 17

OCCUPATION TYPES IN THE PITB, BY SEX

| Sex | Occupations likely to be found in traditional societies | Occupations likely to be found in industrialized societies | Occupations common to both types of societies | |
|------|------|------|------|------|
| Male | 27% (105) | 24% (94) | 49% (192) | 100% (391) |
| Female | 44% (32) | 17% (12) | 39% (28) | 100% (72) |

Chi-square = 48.7
df = 2
Level of Significance = .001

in the labor market. Obviously, this restructuring has not occurred in the Indian textbooks.

## RANGE AND DIVERSITY OF OCCUPATIONS IN THF PITB

### *Traditional Occupational Role Model*

Before discussing our findings on the range and diversity of occupations in the PITB, we shall touch briefly on the traditional occupational role model. The following quote succinctly states its basic assumptions:

Man with his superior physical strength can better undertake the more strenuous tasks, such as lumbering, mining, quarrying, land clearance and house-building. Not handicapped, as is woman, by the physiological burdens of pregnancy and nursing, he can range farther afield to hunt, to fish, to herd, and to trade. Woman is at no disadvantage, however, in lighter tasks which can be performed in or near the home, e.g., the gathering of vegetable products, the fetching of water, the preparation of food, and the manufacture of clothing and utensils. All known societies have developed specialization and cooperation between the sexes roughly along this biologically determined line of cleavage... The advantage inherent in a division of labor by sex presumably account for its universality (Murdock, 1965: 7-8).

The traditional occupational role model distinguishes between males and females on the basis of their ascribed biological "nature." Only by complementing the male does the female serve her "true" or intended function, find fulfillment and realize her "natural" potential. A female's work in the traditional model is thus an extension of her subordinate social role, not vice-versa.

Women made the family's clothes at home and did so in the factory. They nursed the sick at home and did so in the hospitals. They took care of their own houses and other people's houses as domestics. Even today, a very high proportion of all women operatives are engaged in occupations that are traditionally feminine in this sense (Oppenheimer, 1975: 317-318).

In the past, Murdock's data on subsistence activities (Table 18) were often used to explain and justify the "natural" inevitability of sex-based division of labor. Most proponents of such usage conveniently ignored the fact that Murdock's oft-cited compilation of sex-based economic activities in 224 societies was limited to a selection from the Yale University Cross Cultural Survey Files. He did not select his sample from the pool of about 4,000 distinct human cultures with established rules for the division of labor by sex.

Yet, ironically, Murdock's data also illustrate how the traditional androcentric occupational role model is more mythical than factual. As evident in Table 18, the only jobs done exclusively by men in all cultures were hunting animals and pursuing sea mammals. Every other task could be done, in one culture or another, by males, by females, or by both. Although male and female activities seem to cluster in most cultures, exclusive sex-based clustering is applicable only to the two activities cited above. In all other tasks, the presumed universal sex role-based exclusion is absent. For example, though burdens are carried exclusively by men in 12 cultures, it is an exclusively female task in 57 cultures. Only men do the fishing in 98 cultures, but in 4 cultures that is a task exclusively for women. Although women always cook, carry water, and grind grain in most cultures, there are exceptions. In some cultures, these tasks are assigned exclusively to men. Neither does physiology appear to be significant in

determining who does what tasks. The physiological limitations
ascribed to the female have not excluded her from heavy labor

TABLE 18

CROSS-CULTURAL DATA FROM 224 SOCIETIES ON SUBSIS-
TENCE ACTIVITIES AND DIVISION OF LABOR BY SEX

| Activity | Men always | Men usually | Either sex | Women usually | Women always |
|---|---|---|---|---|---|
| | *Number of Societies in which Activity is Performed by:* | | | | |
| Pursuit of sea mammals | 34 | 1 | 0 | 0 | 0 |
| Hunting | 166 | 13 | 0 | 0 | 0 |
| Trapping small animals | 128 | 13 | 4 | 1 | 2 |
| Herding | 38 | 8 | 4 | 0 | 5 |
| Fishing | 98 | 34 | 19 | 3 | 4 |
| Clearing land for agriculture | 73 | 22 | 17 | 5 | 13 |
| Daily Operations | 17 | 4 | 3 | 1 | 13 |
| Preparing and planting soil | 31 | 23 | 33 | 20 | 37 |
| Erecting and dismantling Shelter | 14 | 2 | 5 | 6 | 22 |
| Tending fowl and small animals | 21 | 4 | 8 | 1 | 39 |
| Tending and harvesting crops | 10 | 15 | 35 | 39 | 44 |
| Gathering shellfish | 9 | 4 | 8 | 7 | 25 |
| Making and tending fires | 18 | 6 | 25 | 22 | 62 |
| Bearing burdens | 12 | 6 | 35 | 20 | 57 |
| Preparing drinks and narcotics | 20 | 1 | 13 | 8 | 57 |
| Gathering fruits, berries, nuts | 12 | 3 | 15 | 13 | 43 |
| Gathering fuel | 22 | 1 | 10 | 19 | 89 |
| Preservation of meat and fish | 8 | 2 | 10 | 14 | 74 |
| Gathering herbs, root, seeds | 8 | 1 | 11 | 7 | 74 |
| Cooking | 5 | 1 | 9 | 28 | 158 |
| Carrying water | 7 | 0 | 5 | 7 | 119 |
| Grinding grain | 2 | 4 | 5 | 13 | 114 |

Source: Roy D'Andrade, "Sex Differences and Cultural Institutions,"
in *The Developmeut of Sex Differences*, ed. Elennor E. Maccoby (Stanford:
Stanford University Press, 1966), p. 177.

in agriculture, construction and industry in the U.S.S.R., Asia, Africa and Latin America.

### Deviations from the Traditional Model

We counted a total of 463 occupations for the male and female characters in the PITB. Of these, 84% (N=391) were filled by males while 16% (N=72) were filled by females. A similar distribution emerges in the frequency scores which total 2,081 for all occupations (Appendix G). Males receive 85% N=1,761) of this total, while females receive the remaining 15% (N= 320).

If membership in an occupation is treated as a crucial component of meaningful social identity, this count reflects a heavy bias against females. The female is not only deprived of membership in most occupations, but even the frequency of occupations available to her is modified to uphold the discrepant opportunity structure.

To further examine the deviation from the sex-based occupational model, we divided the total count of PITB occupations into three lists: 1. Occupations assigned *both to the male and female*, 2. Occupations assigned *only to the male* and 3. Occupations assigned *only to the female*. Table 19 lists occupations assigned both to the male *and* female characters in the PITB.

In Table 19, many high-prestige occupations are common to both males and females. As gods, goddesses, holymen, holywomen, and gypsies, both sexes guide and manipulate divine forces. As members of the feudal nobility, they appear as kings, queens, lords, ladies, courtiers and court ladies. Members of both sexes appear as governors, political leaders, prime ministers and army commanders. As professionals, both are represented among medical doctors, priests, social workers, warriors, professors, scholars, scientists, mathematicians, teachers, artists, writers, and students. In the service and production industries, both sexes appear as trade-apprentices, farmers, milk-deliverers, soldiers, laborers, farmworkers, tailors, cooks, weavers and street-hawkers. Of the few low-prestige occupations, males and females are jointly represented as beggars, cooks, shepherds, servants and slaves.

But, when one examines the frequency scores for common occupations, Table 19 loses most of its positive impact. First, the common occupations represent only a meager 13% of the total PITB occupations. Further, while the frequency scores for males are consistently high, the female scores for a given occupation seldom exceed the number 8. Sure there are male and female governors, but the male governors have a frequency score of 8, while the females score only 1. The three high frequency female occupations are held more by the virtue of ascription than achievement. Just as a lowly Maidservant (27) may have accomplished very little to qualify for her position, a Queen's/Princess' status is generally ascribed to her because she is the wife/daughter of a king. This ascription/achievement dichotomy becomes even more discrepant when we categorize the Queen-as-ruler separately. Occupation Queenruler has a frequency of 3, thus singularizing the ascriptive status of the 27 other lessons where women are merely king's wives. The comparative male-female frequency scores in Table 12 do not indicate any movement towards equality between the sexes. At best, the list of common occupations is a catalog of tokenism.

## Occupations Assigned only to the Male

A wide range of 343 occupations are assigned exclusively to the male characters in the PITB. This list, by itself, provides little evidence of its significance. To understand its impact, we must compare it to the list of occupations assigned only to the female.

## Occupations Assigned only to the Female

Twelve occupations are assigned exclusively to the female. These are:

Cleaningwoman, dancer, dietician, housewife, landlady, matron, nun, nurse, pathologist, prostitute, reverend mother, sweeper (N=12).

Of these, only the occupations of the Reverend Mother and to a limited degree, that of the nun involve the exercise of leadership or power over others. In other all cases, the female provides a service through professional occupations. All high-skill professions assigned only to the female fall in the field of health-care, i.e., dietician, nurse, and pathologist.

The remaining occupations assigned only to the female are essentially low-prestige, semi-professional jobs that neither

TABLE 19

FREQUENCY OF OCCUPATIONS COMMON TO BOTH MALES *AND* FEMALES
IN THE PITB; DESCENDING ORDER OF FREQUENCY SCORES

| Males | | Females | |
| --- | --- | --- | --- |
| 89 King | 9 Peasant | 30 Queen | 1 Fairyqueen |
| 52 Soldier | 8 God | 27 Maidservant | 1 Farmworker |
| 44 Servant | 8 Governor | 24 Princes | 1 Godfairy |
| 43 Student | 8 Lord | 8 Student | 1 Governess |
| 42 Doctor, Medical | 8 Shepherd | 6 Leader, Political | 1 Governor |
| 42 Teacher | 8 Washerman | 4 Farmer | 1 Gypsy |
| 36 Prince | 7 Holyman | 4 Goddess | 1 Marchioness |
| 30 Poet | 7 Scholar | 4 Witch | 1 Milliner's Apprentice |
| 28 Farmer | 6 Commander Army | 3 Cook | 1 Minister, Political |
| 28 Writer | 6 Saint | 3 Poet | 1 Priest |
| 27 Priest | 6 Tailor | 3 Queenruler | 1 Prime Minister |
| 19 Leader, Political | 5 Duke | 3 Teacher | 1 Professor |
| 19 Scientist | 5 Farmworker | 3 Writer | 1 Pupil |
| 18 Minister, Political | 4 Beggar | 2 Holywoman | 1 Saint |
| 15 Laborer | 4 Pupil | 2 Housekeeper | 1 Scholar |
| 13 Traveler | 3 Artist | 2 Kitchenmaid | 1 Scientist |
| 12 Professor | 3 Milkman | 2 Lady-Lordwife | 1 Scullion |
| 12 Warrior | 3 Streethawker | 2 Nanny | 1 Seamstress |
| 11 Cook | 3 Weaver | 2 Peasant | 1 Seller, Bangle |
| 11 Prime Minister | 2 Angel | 2 Teacher, Violin | 1 Shepherdess |
| 11 Shopkeeper | 1 Apprentice | 1 Artist | 1 Slave |

11 Slave
10 Courties
1 Gypsy
1 Social Worker
1 Teacher, Music
1 Warlock

1 Beggar
1 Commader Army
1 Court Lady
1 Dealer, Hair
1 Deliverer, Milk
1 Doctor, Medical
1 Duchess
1 Factory Worker
1 Fairy

1 Social Worker
1 Soldier
1 Teacher, Deaf
1 Traveler
1 Warrior
1 Washerwoman
1 Weaver

require extensive training nor bring substantial rewards. As a
cleaning woman, sweeper or landlady, the female works in dull,
dead-end jobs. Even in nursing, a skilled profession, the role
expectations and institutional hierarchy are geared to an occupational pattern of subservience. The role of the nurse, for
example, is perceived more as an extension of the traditional
feminine caring role than as an acquired, performance-oriented,
marketplace specialization.

"No nation can be free," Lenin wrote, "when half the population is enslaved in the kitchen" (Oakley, 1976: 222). As it
happens, most females in the PITB appear as housewives
(frequency score-118). They are assigned an occupation that defines their total identity in terms of domesticity. The non-work
status of the housewife's occupation is too well known to need
any documentation. More dangerous is such enhancement of
housewifery as the most appropriate occupation for females,
which in turn may inhibit achievement-oriented learning among
Indian girls. As Hollingsworth (1922) remarked:

> There seems to be no occupation which supports feeble-
> minded men as well as housework and prostitution support
> feebleminded women. . .The girl who cannot compete. . .may
> drop into the non-competitive vocational life of the household,
> where she naturally performs many routine tasks, requiring
> but rudimentary intelligence. . .

Perhaps as a tribute to the power of partriarchy, prostitution
is also listed as a female occupation in Indian textbooks. In a
society that treats prostitution as both illegal and immoral,
a textbook for impressionable young is a rather awkward place
to find this occupation assigned to the female.

### OCCUPATIONAL PRESTIGE SCORING

One could argue that the frequency of male occupations is higher
because there are more male (N=3076) than female (N=722)
characters in our sample. To double-check, we used the prestige
scores of occupations in the PITB as our second test for inequi-
ties. We presumed occupational prestige ranking to indicate the
degree of deference, acceptance and derogation which a society

attributes to the holders of an occupation.

## Methodology

For scoring, we used the Treiman (1975) International Occupational Prestige Scale. Though Trieman's scale is not the final solution to the problems of cross-societal occupational comparison, its occupational prestige scores are standardized enough for meaningful comparisons.

In Treiman's scale, all occupational prestige scores are assigned on a scale of 1 to 100, with a high score reflecting a higher level of occupational prestige. The methodology for computing mean scores and for scoring occupations not found in Treiman's list is discussed in Appendix D. Since the difference between means of Lesson Prestige Scores and Occupational Prestige Scores was insignificant, we have cited Occupational Prestige Scores means in the following analysis. Both these scores are given in Appendix H.

## Male and Female Occupational Prestige Scores: A Comparison

As shown in Appendix H, the mean occupational prestige scores for males were consistently higher than those for females, regardless of the language, author's sex,[1] prescribing agency, grade level, type or origin of the lesson.[2]

Between the two languages, the female scores for the English language lists were mostly higher than those for Hindi language lists.[3] A comparison of the male and female occupational prestige scores confirmed the weak but noticeable tendency on the part of female authors to give female characters a more judicious treatment.[4] Table 20 indicates that female authors used male occupations with scores almost as high as those used by male authors. But the female authors also scored female occupations at 49, while the average for female occupations was 44 in lessons written by male authors. For reasons discussed in Chapter VI, the female scores were comparatively higher in the biography lesson, yet still not as good as the male scores (Table 23). The difference between biography and non-biography scores was higher in Hindi lessons than it was in English lessons, a difference accounted for by the higher number of biographies in Hindi lessons.

TABLE 20

MEAN OCCUPATIONAL PRESTIGE SCORES, MALE AND
FEMALE BY AUTHOR'S SEX

|  | Author's Sex | | | |
|  | *Male* | *Female* | *Male & Female* | *Indeterminable* |
|---|---|---|---|---|
| Male | 55 | 54 | 47 | 55 |
| Female | 44 | 49 | 40 | 53 |

TABLE 21

MEAN OCCUPATIONAL PRESTIGE SCORES, MALE AND
FEMALE BY AGENCY

|  | Agency | | | | | | |
|  | *Central Board* | *Haryana* | *Kuru-kshetra* | *NCERT* | *Punjab* | *Rajasthan* | *U.P.* |
|---|---|---|---|---|---|---|---|
| Male | 52 | 60 | 57 | 56 | 48 | 56 | 54 |
| Female | 43 | 55 | 46 | 41 | 38 | 48 | 47 |

TABLE 22

MEAN OCCUPATIONAL PRESTIGE SCORES, MALE AND
FEMALE BY GRADE LEVEL

|  | Grade Level | | |
|  | *High School* | *Higher Secondary* | *Prep/Pre-Universtty* |
|---|---|---|---|
| Male | 53 | 54 | 57 |
| Female | 46 | 46 | 46 |

TABLE 23

MEAN OCCUPATIONAL PRESTIGE SCORES, MALE AND
FEMALE BY KIND OF LESSON

|  | Kind of Lesson | |
|  | *Biography* | *Non-Biography* |
|---|---|---|
| Male | 61 | 52 |
| Female | 53 | 43 |

TABLE 24

MEAN OCCUPATIONAL PRESTIGE SCORES, MALE AND<br>FEMALE BY LESSON ORIGIN

|  | Origin | |
|---|---|---|
|  | Indian | Non-Indiau |
| Male | 56 | 53 |
| Female | 47 | 43 |

Both male and female received the highest score in the text-books of Haryana. It is surprising, however, to discover that among agencies, NCERT appeared most sexist, as its textbooks reflected a difference of 15 points (Male=56, Female=41) between male and female occupational prestige scores (Table 21).

*Salience Scores*

The assignment of high scores to males and low scores to females is also apparent in the mean salience scores for male and female occupation lists. The salience score for an occupation was calculated by multiplying its frequency with its occupational prestige score. The mean score for a given list was calculated by dividing its total salience scores by the number of occupations in it. The mean salience score is 55 for the male list and 46 for the female list (Appendix G).

*Concluding Remarks*

*Overall, none of the categories make much difference to the consistently lower prestige scores assigned to the female.* If, using the high-low dichotomy, we take the score of 50 as our dividing point, only 13% of the female occupational prestige scores fall *above* the score of 50. For the male, the situation is exactly the opposite. Only 7% of the male prestige scores lie *below* the score of 50. Thus while 87% of all prestige scores assigned to the female are low in prestige, 93% of all scores assigned to the male are high in prestige. *There is a strong negative correlation between the male and female prestige scores.*

The classic myth of the sex-based division of labor functioned to relegate females to domestic, non-marketplace, low-prestige, low-income occupations as their "natural" and "necessary" vocations. The authors and editors of the PITB, too, have made no effort to enhance the availability of marketplace occupational roles models for the females of today's India.

Nothing could be more unfair to the millions of girls who sit in Indian classrooms just as the boys do. They read the same textbooks, take similar examinations and are expected to develop similar talents for success in the marketplace. Yet when Indian textbooks impart dissimilar occupational aspirations to the two sexes, the young Indian women are most likely to end up as the victims of segregated socialization into stunted selves. Currently, the Indian textbooks encourage their readers to believe that women need not pursue a life independent of or even parallel to their traditioual roles of wife, mother and housekeeper. To foster such exclusion of one half of India's potential contributors is not only a waste of human talent; it is also a denial of the equalitarian ideals to which our country was dedicated.

Hoping that the PITB would expose and contradict the out-dated notions about "man's" and "woman's" work, we had hypothesized:

H-12. As compared to the traditionally sexist division of labor, the range and diversity of occupations in the PITB will be similar for both males and females.

Instead, we find that the Indian textbooks exhibit a division of labor frighteningly close to that of feudal societies. The occupational role modeling in the PITB generally precludes the female from membership in high-skill, high-income, high-prestige occupations. Hypothesis 12 is rejected.

FOOTNOTES

[1]The scores dropped below the means for both languages only in two categories. The score for male and female author category is 47 in English language lessons. In the Hindi lessons authored by females, the score is 43.

[2]We did not see more than a 3-point difference between lessons with Indian and non-Indian origins. In the grade level by language distribution of male occupational prestige scores, the males score lowest in the Hindi high school texts (score=52) and highest in the pre-university lessons (score=60). This 8 point spread is cut in half in both language lists and becomes equal for higher secondary and pre-university lessons (both scores=57).

[3]The female scores highest in the Haryana English lessons (score= 68), and in the both languages category (score=55) for Haryana. In the language by agency distribution, the female occupations score highest in the English lessons. The English textbooks also assign the female a higher than Hindi scoring in all the three grade levels, while the lowest prestige score for the female in grade level by language distribution occurs in the Hindi high school books (scores=36). However, the difference between Hindi and English language scores for female occupations diminishes in the both languages category, where all the three grade level female scores are placed at a close range.

This discrepancy of scores between biographies and non-biographies, noted earlier, continues in the female scores. The females score highest in English biographies (score=55). In the lesson's origin category, female scores are higher in lessons of Indian origin.

[4]The sex of the author does not seem to affect the prestige scores assigned to female occupations by male and female authors. Only the female authors in Hindi have male characters with low prestige scores. But otherwise the difference between the prestige scores assigned by male and female authors in the Hindi and English language categories is negligible. The female occupations get a high score of 53 in the category of anonymous authors in the English language lessons. The difference between the score of 53 and other scores in the author's sex by language distribution represents a significant spread. But since the category by definition, does not tell us anything about the sex of its authors, we cannot use this score to interpret the significance of author's sex.

Does female authorship lead to a restraining influence on the consistently high scoring of male actors by the male authors? The data do not provide a clear answer. The female authors writing in English use male occupations that score even higher than those used by males writing in English. The sudden drop of more than 10 points to 43 in the Hindi female author category for male scores only hints at the possibility of female authors having a minor editorial effect on the uniform inequality between our male and female scores.

Another comparison between the actual scores assigned to the female occupations by the male and female authors, however, reveals an interesting difference. The female authors use female occupations with a higher prestige score. While both male and female authors treat the male occupations in a similar manner, the female authors seem to be more sympathetic to female occupations. A female author treating female occupations seems less likely to saddle the female characters with low prestige occupations.

# CHAPTER IX

# The Traditional (Pre-Independence) and the Post-Independence (PITB) Sex Role Models: A Comparison

To compare the sex role model in PITB with the traditional model, we have organized the following discussion in two sections: 1. Comparison of themes indicative of sex role equality, and 2. Comparison of themes indicative of sex role inequality.

## THEMES INDICATIVE OF SEX ROLE EQUALITY IN THE TWO MODELS

As in the traditional model, the textbooks of independent India draw upon the dominant Vedic ideals as sources for sex role equality. The customary godmother image presents the female as the personification of life-giving forces. Hindu mythology, both in the Great Tradition and the Little Tradition, had elevated the female to the status of *Bhuvaneshwari*, Ruler of the Universe. or the *Graama Maata*, the protector of the villages. The PITB quote the oft-cited injunction that the gods reside where woman are worshipped (08:158).

The PITB also sustain the traditional reverence for motherhood. The Pandava brothers are referred to as their mother's sons (as Kunti's son or Madri's son). Though identifying a son by his mother's name may be no more than a functional device to categorize the offspring of a king with too many wives and too many children, it does elevate the status of motherhood (L-036). One story enhances the old Indian custom of addressing as mother any female who is not personally related. Birbal meets a beautiful woman at night on the outskirts of the city.

Unlike the Western hero meeting the damsel-in-distress at the midnight hours, he entertains no sensual thoughts. Instead, he addresses her as mother (L-034).

Choice of spouse is another right shared by women in the traditional model with some of those in the PITB. In the textbooks, various females choose their own partners, with or without the consent of their parents. When Savitri chooses Satyavan and her father objects to the choice, she simply asserts that she has chosen the man whom she will marry (L-035). A prince, while departing with his beloved on a magic horse, advises her other suitor, "O Sultan of Kashmir, next time you wish to marry a princess, make sure to get her consent first" (21:70).

In both the models, various females appear as significant achievers devoted to noble goals. In the traditional model, the male was more likely to be trained in a formal setting for a marketplace occupation. The PITB shows both males and females enrolled in schools and colleges.

## THEMES INDICATIVE OF SEX ROLE INEQUALITY IN TWO MODELS

The themes indicative of sex role inequality can be divided into two broad sections:1) themes that contribute to gender-based male dominance and 2) themes that institutionalize inequality by characterizing females as an inferior social group.

### Male Dominance

The traditional model required the ideal Indian wife to treat her husband as the polestar of her existence. The PITB do not consider servitude to a husband to be either improper or debasing (L=033). Desdemona, once married, becomes the victim of her husband's possessiveness and dies as a result of her devotion to him. More than one lesson advise how important a husband is. A wife ". . . can give her life for him. But she cannot even imagine a situation where she might hurt him in order to placate somebody else. If she does so, she is a sinner" (34:220). Fine sentiments. But why detail such injunctions for the female alone? How about the husband? Is he only the recipient of such loyalty? Why not spell out his obligations as well? To be fair, the son in a lesson does refuse to go back to his mother unless she accepts the daughter-in-law. But the righteousness of the son is implied, not stated. Nowhere does the author consider it necessary to verbalize his duties as a husband. As in other lessons, only the female's role obligations are spelled out.

There are two stories by Mannu Bhandari in our sample. A prolific writer, she has written many stories that depict the female's rebellion against unfair treatment in a male-dominated society. The editors of Indian texts have chosen to ignore such stories. They have instead chosen, in both instances, stories that portray ideal Hindu females who would rather suffer than rebel against oppression. Anandi, the heroine of a story by Mannu Bhandari, slaves all her life to fulfill the ideal of absolute devotion to her husband (L=344). So effective is her socialization into the subservient role, that she displays no outrage as her inconsiderate husband maltreats her for decades. Why doesn't she rebel? The plot offers no clue besides the implicit assumption that, as an ideal Hindu wife, she must serve her husband for as long as he lives.

The traditional sex role model presumed that the female's primal concern for the males in her life would overrule any awareness of emotional and economic exploitation. To the female in the PITB model, the familial bondage is so strong that no amount of disaparagement can make her choose a path of independence from the male. Instead she is socialized into feeling guilty about pursuing any other interests, be they personal or professional.

Anabel Williams-Ellis, the author of Marie Curie's biography, epitomizes this guilt in her closing comment on the changing status of female scientists.

They do get proper laboratories to work in, they do get paid enough to live on and there are so many of them. It's still difficult for them to manage their babies properly and still go on finding out, but, all the same, quite a lot of them do both jobs very well (20:71).

The statement smacks of a patronizing attitude that conveys a sense of wonder at the ability of the female to do anything scientific. It also supports the typical notion that a female cannot pursue occupations outside her home without somehow endangering the care of her babies. At no time does the author express any dissatisfactton with the lack of proper facilities that should, by now, be rightfully available to female scientists, freeing them from the role-burdens of home maintenance and child care. Here is a naivete implying gratitude for the token facilities. That these niggardly treatments may have deprived many a woman scientist from realizing her full potential does not seem to brother the author at all.

As in the traditional model, the *sarvagunasampanna maryaa-daapurush*—strong, handsome, generous, achieving—males dominate in the PITB model. There are a few henpecked males in the school textbooks of independent India. One story, for example, depicts a male as a droop-shouldered, underweight dandy. While such stereotypes imply the dominance of the female, they also foster contempt for her by suggesting that a powerful woman is also a castrator. Generally, in both models, the strong, responsible males command, support and protect the womenfolk. Even when females may be included in plot, they are generally relegated to supporting roles. When males are present, a plot is most often dominated by men and boys. As "masters" in their homes, most males in the PITB consider it unnecessary to consult the females on household affairs (L—247). When male and female actors in a play disagree with each other, only the female is chastised for disagreeing with the males (L—271). The males' right to disagree with each other is presupposed.

In the traditional model, a female was trained for self-abnegation from early childhood. The PITB in ambivalent on how the males and females should be trained for their later lives as husbands and wives. There is, however, ample support for the desirability of female subservience in the PITB. Often the women accept subservience without question, for no alternatives exist. In dealing with Mr. Tulliver, Mrs. Tulliver has one principle: never oppose him. No wonder, instead of admiring independent and clever Maggie, she admires subservient Lucy as the "perfect daughter" (L—327).

By including such sexist play, both the traditional and the PITB models augment the belief that males qualify, by birthright, to be placed ahead of half the human race. The most frequent victim of this superiority complex is, of course, the female. Maggie's brother Tom says that girls can't learn Latin (while *he* can) an opinion that his headmaster is quick to second. Tom also informs Maggie that, because he's a boy, he has more money than she has. A husband who considers it beneath himself to discuss art with his wife makes perfunctory remarks merely to avoid trouble (7:92).

The PITB plots portray an exaggerated view of male power. Much like the cruel prescriptions of Manu, the female in the PITB is physically punished for her deviation from the traditional roles. Males often use violence as an instrument for asserting their power over women and children. Husbands beat their wives to obtain money, to vent their frustrations, to establish their territorial imperative. And once the husband is gone, widows are particularly victimized for any attempt at independence. No wonder "every Hindu woman prays to die before her husband" (36:6).

Accompanying the female's victimization, the traditional ill-favor for daughters and a declared perference for sons continues unabated in the PITB. One of Savitri's wishes is to have many sons (L—320). Prem Chand, the celebrated novelist, says of his life's ambitions and ideals of achievement: "I have no big plans for my two boys. All I want is that they become honest, truthful and dedicated" (14:52). Prem Chand has a daughter, yet he makes no mention of what he would like for her. When a little girl insists that he must have a brother to celebrate *rakshaabandhan*, her mother chides her: "You put us in the soup we are in. Your birth brought a fatal curse upon your father. Your brother had to leave home by the time you were three years old. You are the one responsible for all these misfortunes inflicted upon the family" (41:80). The mother's reproach is rooted in the folk belief that girls are the harbingers of bad luck, a notion the PITB do not contradict.

While all males are not born lucky in Indian textbooks, they can better insure the realization of their aspirations, even if they must back their authority with physical strength. The feudal code of honor wallpapered a model masculinty, bloodied by expectations of aggressive virility. Such traditions appear intact in the PITB model. In a story set in an all-boy school, the boys test their new teacher by pitting him against the local Hercules in a boxing match. The teacher wins the bloody match, and his superiority is established. The teacher's victory is his passport to acceptance in this male subculture and by implication, in the male world (L-138). Only after an applicant convinces his interviewers of talent as a rugby player is he admitted into a medical school (L—333). Apparently, adeptness at masculine sports is a recommendation for success in other areas, including medicine.

Various males in the PITB seek to dominate the attention of their beloveds and become violenty jealous if the attention is divided. A young sculptor demands that his fiancee abandon her career. She refuses, declaring that marriage cannot usurp her passion for dance (L—45). To prevent her from dancing, he casts a spell on her. He makes a statue in her likeness and breaks the statue's feet. Now she will never dance again: The lesson implies that sorcery can work wonders on a stubborn bride-to-be, and that no means of persuasion is too violent or devious for a passionate male. The story never explains why the sculptor can maintain his artistic career, while his future wife must surrender hers.

In literature of the post-Vedic era particularly the Indian female was normatively male-dependent, homebound and subservient. This tradition continues in the PITB model. Various young girls depend upon their fathers not only for economic support but also for guidelines on how far to study and whom to marry. The nature of male support determines a woman's social existence. She appears helpless when no or only limited male support is available. Princesses and housewives appear as imbeciles incapable of handling simple day-to-day affairs. One woman, her arms loaded down with parcels, can't get a taxi to stop for her. Yet a nearby male merely whistles to summon a fleet of taxicabs (L—141).

Women, unlike men, are encouraged to stay at home. Purdah is considered a symbol of honor. "The girls could go out of the house, for chores, up to the age of four or five. After that, the honor of the family required that they stay in" (33:104). To make such confinement palatable, the traditional and the PITB models either ignore the marketplace achievements of women or use different standards of role performance to define success for females. While mentioning various inventions in technology during the later half of the nineteenth century, an author credits men alone for scientific achievement (L—044). In the essay "Courage" (L—330) a female author cites only male achievers for their self-sacrifice, bravery, generosity or honesty. The only female mentioned in the lesson is a hen, cited not for bravery but for compliance.

In the traditional model, home maintenance was considered the major responsibility of females. The modern Indian textbooks also judge a female's success by her proficiency at household chores. "Supposing you learn plain cooking," advises one character. "That's a useful accomplishment which no woman should be without" (18:177). "Oh, a wondeful pudding!," says Bob Cratchit, regarding it as Mrs Cratchit's greatest success since their marriage (18:226). In a dramatization based on fantasy, various characters from children's book—Alice, Huck Finn, Tom Sawyer—come alive and recite ambitions and dreams which strongly reinforce the sex-role stereotypes. The female characters hope for good husbands, angelic children, and a life of staying at home to take care of the family. A female character states:

> (Dreamily) I should like a lovely house full of all sorts of luxurious things,—nice food, pretty clothes, handsome furniture, pleasant people, and heaps of money. I am to be mistress of it, and manage it as I like with plenty of servants, so I never need work a bit (17:5).

The male characters want to undertake hazardous voyages on the sea, indulge in experimental adventures and become famous for their creativity. A male character states:

> I want to do. . . something heroic or wonderful that wouln't be forgotten after I'm dead. I don't know what, but I'm on the watch for it, and mean to astonish you all some day. I shall write books and get rich and famous . . .(17:6).

Such sex based differences in expectations of performance would doom a competent female to act behind the scene, as in the case of Portia, and force her to narrow the scope of her ambition. The female author/narrator of the lesson, "I Wish I Were a Man" (L-141), counts the advantages and disadvantages of being female. Although she begins by lamenting the disadvantages for a female in a man's world, she concludes that they are small payment for the privileges women enjoy as the recipients of male chivalry. Such an assertion of the female's "privileged" status subjects readers to a double standard which aims to please the female by giving her token respect, while depriving her of any critical leverage in the power structure. The author's ignorance of this inequity and her total disregard for realistic dilemmas which confront women are not as pathetic as her complacent acceptance of subservience as a prized possession.

Also, the female's envy of the male in the Indian textbooks focuses on trivia *par excellence.* She may envy the male because he has more pockets than he would ever need. He never has to worry about setting his hair or keeping up with the latest trends in fashion. The female, on the other hand, is nothing if not well-tailored, made-up and lavishly coiffured. The core of her identity crisis lies in her worries over how to prepare a new dish. The culmination of her achievements is drawn from the compliments she receives from males for her looks and her cooking. The living proof of her good fortune is the fulfillment she realizes in "woman-talk" with her daughters:

> When my husband, with more blind faith than perspicacity, assures me that I am the most charming lady at the party; when my lemon maringue pie emerges from the oven perfect for praise; when my nearly grown-up daughters come to me at night, combing their hair and talking in low voices of the things only women talk about together—then I know what I believed all along is truth. Women are the fortunate people (16:112).

To top it all, the editors of the text (a male and a female) treat these pronouncements as a "rational approach" in their introduction to the lesson! (16:108). When the textbooks propound such behavior as "rational", one can be sure that they would like their readers to grow up as empty-headed, easily-pleased home-bodies, whose aspirations cease at the front door.

Various plots in the PITB place women in the same category with children. Even when disguised as exaltation of females, such categorization amounts to their *de facto* belittlement. After a successful military campaign, one of Shivaji's generals brings back a beautiful Mughal princess as part of the loot (L-298). In the court, Shivaji chastises his general for committing such a violation of decency. Shivaji is reiterating the feudal code of honor: the noble warrior never attacks the old, children and females, even in the enemy's ranks. But note the grouping. The female is inviolable in the classic paradigm because once outside the power structure, she poses no threat. Very much like the old and children, she is not powerful enough to be considered competitive. Hence, she is immune because abusing her will be tantamount to taking advantage of somebody who belongs to a weak and defenseless species.

Often when lumping women with children, weakness is a prime requirement. One story propounds that strong men and soldiers must die to save the weak and children at home. A father tells his son that girls cry, but not boys. In a rescue operation during the loss of Titanic, "many of the women had been hours in those open boats, shielded from the almost arctic cold only by a coat. . .telling of the urgency with which they had left the ship, suggesting to the imagination awful long-drawn-out anxiety before the ships were loosened" (18:156). Why does the author single out only women to describe the anxiety and fear that all the survivors must have experienced? Wouldn't it be more accurate to say "Many of the *people*" rather than just "women?" Is the author trying to imply that women are weaker than men and less capable of bearing hardship? If so, were there significantly more male survivors than female? The lesson never explains.

So many of the qualities ascribed to women have infantile counterparts that the general characterization of the female in the PITB reads like that of an ever-grown child. The female is described as faithless; the child is devoted to self-centered pleasures. She is dependent; the child expects to be cared for. She is manipulative, the child is beguiling. In some cases, she has not even progressed from the irrationality; superstition and foolishness of a spoiled brat.

In its vituperations against females as an inferior species, the traditional model denounced females as despicable, exploitative, evil, foolish, gossipy, ignorant, indulgent, sinister, temperamental, unfaithful, weak and wicked, ad infinitum. Many lessons in the PITB consider the personal flaws in individual females sufficient to constitute a basis for stigmatizing them as a group. Nowhere do the editors of PITB preface the adaptations of classic literary works with any explanation of why the language and plots of traditional literature are outmoded. For example,

Shakespearian characters in lessons based on his plays substantiate Manu's belief that women are faithful only when they have to be. Hamlet's mother schemes to murder her husband and then marries her conspirator brother-in-law. Goneril and Regan epitomize faithlessness. They both love men other than their husbands, and they hold no loyalty to their father or sister (L-239, 240, 241, 242). While talking to a male, the Man in Asbestos describes women as being exploitative. "She did not work. . .half of what you had was hers," he says. "She had the right to live in your house and use your things. At any moment [she] could inveigle you into one of those contracts" (17:229).

Sometimes bitch images of adult women as manipulators are applied to young girls, too. In Jainendra Kumar's story *Khel*, a boy topples a little girl's sand creation. She suffers silently (L-270). The author tells us that her reaction is typical of a female who wants to use her silence to embarrass the male. She is not really angry at the insult inflicted upon her. Rather she views it as a perfect opportunity for manipulation. One wonders how the author can ascribe such motives to a young girl unless, of course, he perceives her as a miniature model of the crafty adult female, the castrator.

In less demonic tales, women appear as gossips and meddlers, lacking in rational self-control. A farmer tells young readers that women, gossipy by nature, cannot keep secrets. Sure enough, his wife babbles to villagers that he has found gold and silver coins (03:53). Another lesson describes the conversation of four females as a never-ending stream of chatter about babies, servants, gardens, husbands and clothes (03:18).

Like stereotypic children, the PITB women often act without any sense of logic or reason. In *Sanskar Aur Bhavna*, a play by Vishnu Prabhakar, an orthodox mother disapproves of her son's decision to marry outside the caste (L-313). Though the son is equally responsible for the unorthodox love marriage, only his wife is chastised for taking him away, thus breaking his mother's heart (34:220). In the grand *filmi* tradition, the daughter-in-law is deemed as the source of conflict, the hand that rends the time-honored trilogy of a happy-son-daughter-in-law-widowed-mother scenario.

A disregard for reason characterizes the behavior of other females who are portrayed as either excessively temperamental or downright foolish. To fulfill their sex roles, some women in the PITB resort to superstitious irrationality. Whether from upbringing or need, these women use the supernatural to explain situations in their lives. One woman believes she can conceive a child by performing religious rituals and prayers. Another subscribes to the therapeutic value of witchcraft. Similar beliefs underlie many irrational fears. A mother is apprehensive that, out of jealousy, her barren neighbor will injure her children by witchcraft (L-85). A woman attributes the death of her husband and the disappearance or her son to the ominous birth of her daughter (L-350).

Women in Indian textbooks seem to be crazy about following fashions, even when such fashions are uncomfortable, and impractical, like high heeled shoes. Among Typees, while men undertake activities essential for the survival of their society, the girls idly anoint themselves with fragrant oils, dress their hair and compare their trinkets (19:106).

The PITB is not as blatant as the traditional model in treating the female as chattel, but some role models projected in the PITB do degrade the female to the commodity level. As the story of Mahabharata is narrated in the PITB (L-236), Draupadi ends up serving as the wife of five brothers. Since polyandry was not the custom of the geographical region inhabited by the Pandavas, and since the royal persons of the Great Tradition epics are more often polygamous than polyandrous, Draupadi's case represents the female's humiliation by the male. Her status in the plot is derived from her placement as a prize to the most competent male. Her only and dubious freedom in choosing a marital partner is based on the outcome of a public martial arts competition. Later, she serves as a pawn in ego-games between the Kaurvas and the Pandavas. Much like a possession, she is exposed and knocked around in a gathering of gamblers because her husband "loses" her on a bet. In the climax of the story, her only value is as a prop to justify the war, waged between males, to avenge her honor.

Similar debasement of the female is manifest even in religious lore which originated with good intentions. Although the traditional model projected a spirit of male-female interdependence in the act of Creation, the two parables depicting the Ideal Man and Woman in the PITB, manage to tarnish the pleasant spirit of cooperation represented in the *ardhanaarishwar* concept of divine androgyny. The classic metaphor is so ravaged by sexism that it is hardly recognizable.

"Dasi se Grihalaxmi" by Rajgopalachari attemps to illustrate the complementary relationship between the two sexes (L-065). A man treats his woman like a slave. To make the man realize the importance of the woman, God takes her away but provides the man with the same household services she once supplied. The man feels incomplete. Sensing a change in the man's attitude, God returns the woman. Thereupon, she is worshipped by the man who declares her to be the poetry of his soul and the goddess of prosperity.

Explicitly, this story reinstates the female as the male's "better half." She should not be taken for granted because she is more than the sum total of the services she provides. But the exaltation is curiously hollow. Whether slave or goddess, she is still portrayed as para-human. Constraint, whether physical or emotional, is constraint nonetheless. Throughout the story, all dialogue takes place between the man and God. Nowhere does the author, a male, tell the reader how the woman feels about her treatment, either as slave or goddess. Intensifying her status as an object, she neither does nor says anything which might make the male realize her worth as a person.

Another story, Ugra's "Deshbhakta," opens with a dialogue between the male Creator and his female counterpart (L-352). She asks her "master" if he can make something unique, but when the creator asks if she would like to help him in the process of designing the unique male (what else!), she says, "Ah, come on !...If I really had the ability to create, I would't have bothered you." "But I am not asking you to design or anything of the sort, "he replies, "just sit silently by my side" (41:103).

The readers are likely to perceive the feminine counterpart to the Eternal Creator as a prototype of all females. To assign her a totally inactive role in the act of creation and to treat her as a temperamental, pretty do-nothing is once again to depreciate the female as a passive spectator with a low self-concept. After being exposed to such materials, the young readers are unlikely to dispute the power of males over females. They may very well believe that the woman's castigation is a distasteful but normatively correct treatment.

Thus, in both the models:

1. The proportion of male authors is far higher than of female authors.

2. Males constitute a heavy majority of leading characters.

3. Females are victimized to a greater extent than males. The modes of such sex role victimization include verbal and physical abuse through male-centered language, evaluative degradation, role constrains and actual physical violation.

4. The male is more likely to dominate the decision-making situations. His right to dominate is generally derived from sex-role prerogatives rather than from his problem solving abilities or other functional competency.

5. Both in social and marketplace relationships, the male is more likely to be dominant and cooperative while the female is more likely to be cooperative and subservient.

6. The females in politics do have authority at all levels. But instances of female preeminence in other marketplace authority structures are rare.

7. As subjects of biography, males represent an extremely high proportion of significant actors and achievers in market-place activities.

8. The range and diversity of occupations suggested is narrower for females than for males. Both models exclude the female from performing certain roles/activities because these activities are considered unfeminine, and beyond the capabilities of females.

9. A sexist division of labour is kept intact. The PITB do not depict both males and females as regularly performing non-marketplace activities required to maintain a household, e.g,, cooking, cleaning and washing clothes.

10. Predominantly sexist imagery is used to characterize individuals. Both models portray the sexes not as human beings with common strengths and weaknesses, but as stereotypes with either "masculine" or "feminine" attributes.

## Concluding Remarks

As the preceding discussion shows, the sex-role model in the textbooks of independent India draws upon the worst of the Indian tradition and bastardizes the best of it. In lesson after lesson, the male retains his absolute dominance. As a father, he may bemoan the birth of a daughter, while praising his sons. He may treat her as a commodity, train her for subservience, force her to remain at home, and constrain her freedom to choose a spouse.

Women in the PITB are enslaved to a double standard which promotes different kinds of freedom and achievement potential for the two sexes. Men and women in Indian textbooks do not possess equal property or divorce rights. They are not allowed equal freedom to perform religious rites or to remarry after their spouse had died. Both before and after marriage, the females have less freedom than the males. Marriage is idealized as a communion of unequals. A woman is expected to unquestioningly obey her husband while he lives and then follow him to the pyre when he dies. Even today, the PITB idealize *sutti* and *jauhar*. Presumably, because a woman is little more than chattel, her death is no great loss.

What's more, by uncritically casting females in such submissive and unequal roles, the PITB are encouraging their emulation. Apparently, when it comes to sexism in Indian textbooks, the more things change, the more they remain the same.

# CHAPTER X

# Afterword

So, sexism rules. At the macro-level, it serves to justify social structures that refuse females equal access to legitimate opportunities and rewards in areas where sex is a totally irrelevant criterion. At the micro-level, sexism supports conditions allowing the members of one sex to be socialized into marketplace, achievement-oriented leadership patterns, while conditioning the other sex to seek fulfillment through non-marketplace, supportive roles.[1]

A comparison of the Indian and American textbooks for adolescents illustrates the universality of patriarchal sexism. Research on sexism in American textbooks (Appendix J) indicates that: 1. The traditional stereotype of the active male and passive female persists in the textbooks. 2. The texts continue to reinforce the traditional notions about sex-appropriate activities and attitudes by segregating male characters into "manly" and female characters into "womanly" occupations. 3. The texts not only highlight the males as achievers, but also tend to omit female achievers.

Points 1 and 2 are common to American and Indian textbooks for the young. Females appear as characters less frequently in both American and Indian texts. In the *Women on Words and Images* (1972) analysis of 134 children's readers, the ratio of male biographies to female biographies was six to one. Our Indian sample is similar in the sex composition of its subjects for biographies (male=87%, female=13%, male to female ratio= 6.75:1). Similarly, the male and female characters are not offered a common range of marketplace occupations. A six to one male to female ratio of disparity in total occupations appears in the texts of both countries.[2] Both Indian and American textbooks portray males and females more as traditional stereotypes than as whole human beings. In the textbooks of both countries, men make history, while women do the dishes.

This is particularly appalling in the Indian case because the ideal-type of female as achiever is not considered an aberration in the Indian tradition. A similar ideal does not appear as forcefully in the American tradition where women's accomplishments still go unrecognized among the popular folk and historical literature of America. The Indian female has enjoyed a different status in this respect. Warrior-queens, scholars, politicians and writers have always been known and recognized in common folklore transmitted to Indian children. Indian women actively shared the political burden in the war for independence from the British. And the majority of Indians are not that far from endorsing equal rights. In a survey conducted by the Indian Institute of Public Opinion, 45% of the urban and 60% of the rural respondents said that women should have the same property rights as men (Sinha, 1970).

Yet the Indian textbooks display a disdainful apathy towards presenting the female as a capable achiever like the male. To date, the ideological monomania of patriarchal sexism has prevented Indian educators from even perceiving the need for equal sex role models in textbooks for the young.

Some may argue that our inclusion of celebrated classics as examples of sexist literature is naive, if not, indeed, profane. India, this argument would run, has a rich cultural heritage. Sure the classics are patriarchal and male-oriented. But should we eliminate our literary heritage from the classroom merely because it is not egalitarian? Is such bowlderizing proper?

Such vapors are over-reactive and short-sighted. By pointing out sexist strains in literature and advocating an end to sexism, we are not suggesting censorship. Nor are we presuming a right to dictate terms to literary creativity. To the contrary, by prescribing sexist textbooks, it is the Indian government and her educators who are dictating that inequality supported in the past need not be challenged today.

At present, sexism travels a circuitous route: the PITB incorporate classics with themes conducive to sex role inequality, ignoring works equal in literary stature but opposed to blatant male dominance. Where are the unadulterated myths of divine androgyny? Where is Ibsen's, *A Doll's House?* The producers of our textbooks (and perhaps most of the Indian schoolteachers) do not expostulate upon the mechanics of male dominance. They also consider it unnecessary to include non-sexist literary works to provide a balanced perspective.

Given the above, our argument is not so much over the fact that some classics are sexist, but rather that they are taught without amplification, thus legitimizing inequality as an ingredient of our cultural heritage. Certainly, the classics are worth studying; certainly, they reflect our heritage. But the heritage *is* patriarchal, and the textbook lessons which highlight this fact alone, unaccompanied by notes or introductions outlining their antiquated historical and ideological context, sanction sexism not only of the past, but also of the present, and even of the future.

Although we have not evaluated every textbook read by every child throughout India, we believe our sample is representative enough to indicate trouble. Since recognition of a problem is the first step toward its solution, we suggest that the Indian government and its educators open their eyes to the cancer we have found degenerating the integrity of the Indian school system.

*Suggestion for Further Research*

Since our sample is taken from North Indian states, a similar analysis of the textbooks in other provisions of India may yield regional variations in sex role characterization. Such analyses would test the applicability of our findings to the rest of the country.

It might also be fruitful to analyze the sex role attitudes of the personnel directly responsible for the content of the PITB: Members of textbook committees at the state and national levels, policy-makers involved with producing textbook materials, editors and writers at agencies like the NCERT, Central Institute of English, etc. Since these people actually produce and approve textbooks, their views may help us learn why the original intent of desexistizing the PITB has not been executed in the last two decades.

## Policy Suggestions

While the PITB are not totally devoid of sex role equalitarianism, their overall stance is decidedly patriarchal, sexist and male-favored. To correct this bias and effectively implement an educational system conducive to sex role equality, we propose the following restatement of our hypotheses:

1. The sex role imagery in the PITB must portray the members of both sexes as whole human beings and not merely in terms of their traditional, stereotypic masculine/feminine attributes.

2. The proportion of male authors in the PITB must not be far higher than that of female authors.

3. As compared to the sexism of traditional linguistic usage, the PITB must not use such nouns or pronouns that exclude females in generalizations about human society or the world.

4. As compared to the predominantly negative role-image of the female in traditional literary stereotypes, the PITB must not foster contempt for women by including anti-feminine statements that degrade women in general.

5. Among the subjects of biography, the PITB must not depict males as representing an extremely high proportion of significant achievers.

6. Among the subjects of biography in the PITB, the parental and marital roles of a female must not be highlighted as more essential to her identity than to the identity of a male.

7. Unlike the traditional sex role-based segregation of a "man's" and a "woman's" work, the PITB must depict both male and female subjects of biograpy as performing marketplace as well as non-marketplace domestic activities.

8. Males must not constitute a heavy majority of leading characters in the PITB.

9. In decision-making situations involving the sexes, the PITB must not depict the male as more likely to dominate the decision-making process, nor should his right to dominate be derived from his sex role prerogatives rather than from his problem-solving abilities or other competency.

10. The PITB must not depict the male as more likely to be dominant-cooperative in social and marketplace authority relationships, while depicting the female as more likely to be

cooperative-subservient.

11. The male and female in the PITB must not be victimized through sex role limitations as manifest in role restraints, evaluative degradation or actual physical violation.

12. As compared to the traditionally sexist division of labor, the range and diversity of occupations in the PITB must be similar for males and females.

We realize that trying to desexistize the Indian cultural milieu is bound to be a painstakingly slow process. But the pace of change can be guided and accelerated by those who cherish the goals of equality between the sexes. It is not enough to go on opening new schools, while the content of classroom instruction continues to be poisoned by a sexist bias. Education must be more thon a one-way street to sustain cultural values which consider what is "masculine" to be somewhat better than what is "feminine". Against such a formidable wall of inequality, how can a woman's motivation to challenge bias in the opportunity structure not be depressed? It is the obligation of Indian schools and citizens to ensure that it not be. After all, the days of "Vive la difference!"[3] are over.

## FOOTNOTES

[1]"Either pattern may be unhealthy, but the feminine pattern is the one which produces a character least compatible with the cultural values of achievement and competitive striving" (Whitehurst, 1977:67).

[2]The Women on Words and Images (1972) study found that men had been assigned 147 jobs (85%), while the women in the same texts occupied only 25 jobs (15%). In our Indian sample we counted a total of 463 occupations. Of these, 391 (84%) belong to the male, while 72 (16%) belong to the female. In the realm of marketplace achievement, the textbooks of both countries appear to relegate females to comparative insignificance.

[3]In the summer of 1975, I attended a talk on the women's role in Indian society, held at the plush Nehru Museum in New Delhi. When, during the discussion period, I tried to point out the dangers of stereotypically differentiated sex role expectations, I received a similar response from Dr. T.N. Madan—an Indian sociologist and the main speaker for the evening.

Appendices

APPENDIX A

# List of Lessons

| | |
|---|---|
| 06—062 | Bure Fanse Mahmaan Ban Kar |
| 06—063 | Sona Aur Mitti |
| 06—064 | Ghar Aai Laxmi |
| 07—065 | Daasi Se Grihalaxmi |
| 07—066 | Kutte Ki Poonch |
| 08—067 | Gautam Buddha |
| 08—068 | Isa Masih |
| 08—069 | Raja Ram Mohan Roy |
| 08—070 | Swami Dayanand Saraswati |
| 08—071 | Lokmanya Bal Gangadhar Tilak |
| 08—072 | Mahatma Gandhi |
| 08—073 | Shantidoot Jawahar Lal Nehru |
| 08—074 | Shanti Ke Pujari: Yudh Ke Devta |
| 08—075 | Gurudev Ravindra Nath Thakur |
| 08—076 | Dr. Zakir Hussain |
| 08—077 | Vigyanacharya Jagdish Chandra Basu |
| 08—078 | Chandrashekhar Venkata Raman |
| 08—079 | Dr. Homi Jahangir Bhabha |
| 08—080 | Maharana Pratap |
| 08—081 | Netaji Subhashchandra Bose |
| 08—082 | Jhansi Ki Rani Laxmibai |
| 08—083 | Indira Gandhi |
| 09—084 | Boodhi Kaki |
| 09—085 | Taai |
| 09—086 | Do Banke |
| 09—087 | Apna-Paraya |
| 09—088 | Maharaja-Ka-Ilaj |
| 09—089 | Sev Aur Dev |
| 09—090 | Sayani Bua |
| 09—091 | Bhola Ram Ka Jiv |
| 09—092 | Bhatakati Rakh |
| 10—093 | Bare Bhai Sahib |
| 10—094 | Mamta |
| 10—095 | Har Ki Jeet |
| 10—096 | Shatru |
| 10—097 | Dwanda |
| 10—098 | Atom Bomb |
| 10—099 | Gunvanti Mausi |
| 10—100 | Naukari Pesha |
| 10—101 | Kaidi |

| | |
|---|---|
| 11—102 | Namak Ka Daroga |
| 11—103 | Ve Svyam Ghulab The |
| 11—104 | Bhulakkar Bhai Sahib |
| 11—105 | Lal Kela |
| 11—106 | Chay Ke Pyale Men Toofan |
| 12—107 | Idgah |
| 12—108 | Pajeb |
| 12—109 | Kamare, Kamara Aur Kamare |
| 12—110 | Kalam-Ke-Sipahi: Upnyas Samrat Premchand |
| 12—111 | Rashtrapati Rajendra Prasad |
| 12—112 | Sabhya Vesh Men |
| 12—113 | Adhikar Ka Rakshak |
| 12—114 | Vapasi |
| 12—115 | Reedh Ki Haddi |
| 13—116 | Ram Ji Ki Cheenti: Ram Ji Ka Sher |
| 14—117 | Khadi Ka Janm |
| 14—118 | Ganv Ka Jeevan |
| 14—119 | Use Na Bhooloonga |
| 14—120 | Svargiya Prem Chand |
| 14—121 | Yug Pravartak Bhartendu Harishchandra |
| 15—122 | The Fifteenth of August |
| 15—123 | Andy Rooney |
| 15—124 | From Balloons to Aeroplanes |
| 41—125 | Sachhi Veerta |
| 15—126 | Raja Jaisingh |
| 15—127 | The Discovery of Penicillin |
| 15—128 | Abu-Hassan |
| 15—129 | Gandhiji as a Lawyer |
| 15—130 | The Mysterious Painting |
| 40—131 | Urree Hui Deevar |
| 16—132 | I Came Back from the Dead |
| 16—133 | A Voyage to Lilliput |
| 16—134 | Fire |
| 16—135 | Tolstoy Farm |
| 16—136 | Shackleton's Greatest Adventure |
| 16—137 | I Meet My Aunt |
| 16—138 | The P.T. Lesson |
| 16—139 | The Light Has Gone Out |
| 16—140 | Adolf |

| | |
|---|---|
| 26—254 | Thomas Alva Edison |
| 27—255 | Sri Rama Krishna Paramahamsa |
| 26—256 | Robin Hood Meets Little John |
| 26—257 | The Pied Piper of Hamlin |
| 26—258 | The Great Pyramid |
| 26—259 | Sindbad the Sailor |
| 25—260 | Jeevan-Gatha |
| 25—261 | Dinbandhu Andrews |
| 25—262 | Lachhma |
| 27—263 | Kerala Ka Sudama |
| 27—264 | Naye Mahmaan |
| 27—265 | Deep Daan |
| 28—266 | Puraskar |
| 28—267 | Kotar Aur Kutir |
| 28—268 | US Kee Maan |
| 28—269 | Nirapad |
| 28—270 | Khel |
| 29—271 | Seema Rekha |
| 29—272 | Maha Manav |
| 29—273 | Swami and his Father |
| 30—274 | Maori Villages |
| 30—275 | Alfred Nobel |
| 30—276 | Monday Morning |
| 30—277 | The Easter Egg |
| 30—278 | On Patrol |
| 30—279 | Columbus Sails |
| 30—280 | The Whirlpool |
| 30—281 | Fighting the Invisible |
| 30—282 | Operation Indian Ocean |
| 32—283 | The Golden Touch |
| 31—284 | Story of Tom Thumb |
| 31—285 | Ilyas |
| 21—286 | The Selfish Giant |
| 31—287 | The Orphans |
| 31—288 | At the Church Door |
| 31—289 | Kindness Rewarded |
| 31—290 | Yudhishthira's Final Trial |
| 31—291 | Handful of Wheat |
| 31—292 | The Lost Child |
| 32—293 | Guru Gobind Singh |

| | |
|---|---|
| 32—294 | Lala Lajpatrai |
| 32—295 | Bharat Kokila Sarojini Naidu |
| 32—296 | Dakshini Dhruv Ka Anveshan |
| 33—297 | Taimur Ki Haar |
| 33—298 | Shiva Ji Ka Saccha Swarup |
| 33—299 | Jonk |
| 33—300 | Kabootar Khana |
| 33—301 | Mangal, Maanav Aur Machine |
| 32—302 | Jurmana |
| 33—303 | Berri |
| 33—304 | Parda |
| 33—305 | Athanni Ka Chor |
| 33—306 | Ashikshit Ka Hriday |
| 33—307 | Gheesa |
| 33—308 | Mandi |
| 34—309 | Swami Vivekanand |
| 34—310 | Lala Lajpat Rai |
| 34—311 | Pariksha |
| 34—312 | Us Ne Kaha Tha |
| 34—313 | Sanskar Aur Bhavna |
| 35—314 | A Spark Neglected Burns the House |
| 35—315 | The Tempest |
| 35—316 | Gulliver in Lilliput |
| 35—317 | The Country of the Blind |
| 34—318 | The Glorious White Washer |
| 35—319 | Michael Goes Climbing |
| 36—320 | Savitri |
| 36—321 | Pratikriya: Ek Jeevan Kasauti |
| 36—322 | The Enchanted Pool |
| 36—323 | A Silver Tongued Orator |
| 36—324 | The Best Loved Man of India |
| 35—325 | Ashoka |
| 36—326 | Duty |
| 37—327 | The Mill on the Floss |
| 38—328 | An Excellent Father |
| 38—329 | Fetching the Doctor |
| 38—330 | Courage |
| 38—331 | The School for Sympathy |
| 38—332 | The Never Never Nest |
| 38—333 | An Interview |

# Dictionary of Favorable Images

**ACCOMMODATING:** Helpful, obedient, adjusting, cooperative, deferential, homely, respectful.

**ACHIEVER:** Builder, conqueror, discoverer, distinguished, victorious, winner, successful, well-off, prominent.

**ADVENTUROUS;** Venturesome, extrovert.

**AGILE:** Active, energetic, vigorous, brisk, lively.

**AMBITIOUS:** A Career-oriented.

**BEAUTIFUL:** Pretty, gracious, lady-like, lovely, good-looking.

**BELOVED:** Precious.

**BRAVE:** Courageous, daring, fearless, bold, unafraid, undaunted, fighter, fierce, gutsy, intrepid, unflinching, warrior, active fighter, Lion of Punjab.

**BRILLIANT:** Bright, child prodigy, genius, eccentric.

**CAREFUL:** Cautious, hesitant, parsimonious, suspicious, taciturn.

**CHEERFUL:** Fun-loving, carefree, lively, easy-going, hearty, joyful, playful, gay, happy.

**CIVIC SPIRITED:** Law-abiding, lawful, public-spirited, public servant.

**CLASSICIST:** Traditionalist, purist.

**CLEVER:** Perspicacious, shrewd, cunning calculating.

**COMMANDING:** Domineering, authoritarian, ruler, dominant, leader, master, masterful, organizer, planner, administrator, expert warrior.

**COMPASSIONATE:** Understanding, considerate, passionate, sensitive, civil, concerned, comforting, thoughtful, sweet, clan-oriented.

**CONFIDENT:** Self-confident, optimistic, self-assured, assured.

**CONTENT:** Self-satisfied.

**CULTURED:** Polished, sophisticated, well-behaved, well-dressed charming, courteous, well-mannered, suave, patron of arts, articulate, particular.

DETERMINED: Persistent, unyielding, full of conviction, strong-willed, resolute, dogged, steadfast.

DEVOTED: Dedicated, devoted worker

DISCIPLINARIAN: Strict, stern, stoic, disciplined, well-organized.

DIVINE: divine messenger, holy,

DUTEOUS: responsible, reliable,

EARNEST: Sincere, eager,

FRIENDLY: Amiable, amicable, convivial, likeable, neighborly encouraging.

GALLANT: Gentlemanly, chivalrous, valiant, sharp dresser.

GENEROUS: forgiving, charitabie, altruistic, benevolent, philanthropic, big-hearted, munificient, placable.

GENTLE: Soft-spoken, soft-heared.

HARDWORKING: Energetic, industrious, ardent, conscientious, diligent.

HEROIC: Great, rescuer.

HONEST: Frank, truthful, blunt, speaker of truth, truth-loving, veracious, veridical, forthright, man of truth, defender of truth, ethical, moral, moralist, candid.

HUMANITARIAN: humanist.

HUMBLE: Modest, penitential, piacular, repentent.

HUMOROUS: Good-humored, jovial.

IDEALIST: Principled.

INDEPENDENT: Freedom-loving, decisive, outspoken, self-made, assertive, self-sufficient, free-spirited, indomitable, self-reliant, self-supporting, argumentative.

INNOCENT: Childlike

INNOVATIVE: Cupious, inventive, creative, initiating, experimental, social reformer, anti-traditionalist, imaginative, investigative, inquisitive,

INSPIRATIONAL: Inspiring.

INTELLIGENT: Perceptive, far-sighted, scientific, keen observer, logical, promising, intellectual.

INTROSPECTIVE: Pensive, visionary.

JUST: Upright, judgmatic, fair, impartial, dispassionate, indiscriminating.

KIND: Gentle, consoling, sympathetic, caring, kind-hearted, non-violent, beneficient, benign, life-saver, merciful, pitying, warm, mild, tender.

LIBERAL: Democratic, tolerant, broad-minded, openminded, progressive, reformist, liberated, feminist.

LOVING: Affectionate.

LOYAL: Trustworthy, grateful, allegiant, pativrata.

NOBLE: Good, virtuous, good-natured, pure, unspoiled luminous, chaste, celibate.

ORATOR: Oratorical, gifted speaker.

PATIENT: Quiet.

PATRIOTIC: Nationalist.

PEACE-LOVING: Pacifist, peaceful.

PERSEVERING: Adamant, convincing tenacious, unbeaten, unwearing, stable.

PERSUASIVE: Convincing.

POLITE: Courteous.

POLITICAL ACTIVIST: Political agitator, revolutionary, political leader.

PRACTICAL: Realistic, pragmatic.

PROUD: Honor-loving, majestic.

RELIGIOUS: God worshipping, pious, believer in God, religiously devoted, god-fearing.

RESPECTED: Respectable, well-esteemed, well-respected, chief guest. honorable, admirable, venerable, honored.

SCHOLARLY: Knowledgeable, learned, well-read, multilingual, great teacher.

SELF-SACRIFICING: Unselfish, Sacrificing, selfless.

SERIOUS: Solemn.

SIMPLE: Ascetic, proletarian, unpretentious, non-materialistic.

SKILFUL: Skilled, competent, efficient, methodical, talented, thorough, good rider, skilled horseman, skilled dancer.

SMART: Quick thinker, alert, business-minded, worldly, common sense, ingenious, quick, fast learner, efficient, prompt, neat.

SPIRITUALIST: Spiritual.

STRONG; Tough, powerful, aggressive, calm, firm, indefatigable, mighty, muscular, sturdy, uncompromising, unconquerable, uncorruptible, well-built, imperturbable, vibrant, tough swimmer, well-made, healthy.

VIGILANT: Watchful.

WISE: Sagacious, experienced, widely-travelled, all-knowing, traveller.

## APPENDIX C

# Biography List

| Actor ID | Name | Occupation |
|---|---|---|
| 001 | Shiva Ji | King Warrior |
| 002 | Dinbandhu Andrews | Author |
| 003 | Admiral Michael Ruyter | Admiral |
| 004 | Horoun Tazieff | Geologist |
| 005 | Hargovind Khorana | Chemist, Research Scientist |
| 006 | Socrates | Philosopher |
| 007 | Sir Winfred Grenfell | Doctor (Medicine) |
| 008 | Ambrosio O'Higgins | Adventurer, Administrator |
| 009 | Roald Amundsen | Adventurer |
| 010 | Gautam Buddha | Prince, Philosopher. Teacher |
| 011 | Jesus Christ | Prophet |
| 012 | Raja Ram Mohan Roy | Religious Leader, Social Reformer |
| 013 | Swami Dayanad Saraswati | Religious Leader, Reformer |
| 014 | Lokmanya Bal Gangandhar Tilak | Journalist, Political Agitator |
| 015 | Mahatma Gandhi | Lawyer, Political Leader |
| 016 | Jawahar Lal Nehru | Politician, Prime Minister |
| 017 | Lal Bahadur Shastri | Politician, Prime Minister |

| 018 | Rabindra Nath Tagore | Poet, Landlord, Educator |
|-----|----------------------|-------------------------|
| 019 | Dr. Zakir Hussain | Teacher, President of Nation |
| 020 | Jagdish Chandra Basu | Scientist |
| 021 | Chandrashekhar Vekanta Raman | Scientist |
| 022 | Dr. Homi Jahangir Bhabha | Scientist |
| 023 | Maharana Pratap | King, Warrior |
| 024 | Netaji Subhash Chandra Bose | Political Leader |
| 025 | Laxmi Bai (Jhansi Ki Rani) | Queen |
| 026 | Indira Gandhi | Prime Minister |
| 027 | Prem Chand | Author, School Inspector |
| 028 | Dr. Rajendra Prashad | President of Nation |
| 029 | Bhartendu Harish Chandra | Poet, Author |
| 030 | Sir Alexander Fleming | Scientist |
| 031 | Albert Einstein | Scientist |
| 032 | Abraham Lincoln | Lawyer, President of Nation |
| 033 | Ashoka, the Beloved of Gods | King |
| 034 | Sir Isaac Newton | Scientist |
| 035 | Charles Dickens | Writer, Novelist |
| 036 | Sir Walter Scott | Author, Poet, Novelist |
| 037 | G. Marconi | Inventor |
| 038 | Helen Keller | Teacher of Deaf |
| 039 | Kasturba | Housewife, Political Leader |
| 040 | Acharya Vinoba Bhave | Social Reformer |
| 041 | Florence Nightingale | Nurse |
| 042 | Louis Pasteur | Scientist, Researcher |
| 043 | Marie Curie | Research Scientist |
| 044 | Thomas Alva Edison | Inventor, Scientist |
| 045 | Ramakrishna Paramhansa | Preacher |
| 046 | Nirala | Poet |
| 047 | Alfred Nobel | Scientist, Inventor |

| 048 | Guru Gobind Singh | Religious Leader |
| 049 | Lala Lajpat Rai | Political Leader |
| 050 | Sarojini Naidu | Poet, Political Leader |
| 051 | Swami Vivekananda | Social Reformer, Preacher |
| 052 | Dr. Alain Bombard | Physician, Explorer |
| 053 | Casteret | Explorer |
| 054 | Professor Piccard | Professor |

# A Note on the Methodology Used for Computing Occupational Prestige Scores in the PITB

All occupations found in the PITB model were not listed in Treiman (1975). To assign comparable scores, we treated occupations not listed in Trieman as such:

When the exact title of an occupation could not be found in Treiman (1975), we tried to locate a comparable unit group or major group where the occupation was most likely to be located. The prestige score for that particular group was then assigned to the specific occupation. E.g., Teacher of the deaf, not specifically mentioned in Treiman (1975), was assigned the unit group score for 0135—Special Education Teachers.

(2) The members of nobility were treated as a group most likely to be responsible for administrative and managerial functions in their societies. God, gods, and godesses were also viewed as dominant managers in their respective spheres of action. All occupations relating to nobility and godlike figures were assigned the major group score of 02 for the Administrative and Managerial workers category. The following occupations were included by this expansion of category 02: archduke, baron, duke, duchess, knight, lord, nobleman, prince, ladylordwife, princess, marchioness, queen, god, god of death, god of harvest, god of water, god of wind, spirit of the waters, goddess. Kings, emperors, pharohs and queen rulers were classified as chiefs-of-state.

(3) The following occupations were assigned the group score for the category of 1300, referring to people NOT in the labor force, but with a source of income: Gentleman, squire, courtier,

courtlady, con man, bandit chief, burglar, outlay, pirate, robber, ruffian, gypsy, traveler.

(4) The following occupations were assigned the group score for category 03101—Minor Civil Servants: informer, spy.

(5) For inventor, leader political, religious leader, adventurer, prophet, revolutionary, social reformer, saint, creator-of-universe, God, we invented a new category —14—and assigned it an arbitrary score of 85. Since most incumbents of occupations included in this category are heroes who had wide-ranging impact on the history of their societies, and the world in general, a score of 85 places them below the score assigned to a chief of state or primeminister, but above the score of a supreme court justice, a general, a governor or a vice-chancellor.

(6) The following occupations were assigned group score for category 014—workers in Religion: astrologer, Brahman.

(7) Occupation-Housewife is not listed in the Indian National Classification of Occupations (1968). The occupational prestige scales for non-western societies do not rate it either. In order to assign a prestige score to the work of a housewife, we had to decide on two main questions: (*i*) Can the work of a housewife be treated as an occupation? (*ii*) If so what prestige score should it be assigned?

(*i*) Since an occupation in industrial societies is considered to be a predominantly marketplace phenomenon, the disregard for the occupation "housewife" may be traced to the traditional dichotomy between the activities that took place inside and outside of the house. Activities within the house were dominantly feminine and considered relatively unimportant, while the activities conducted outside the house (business, politics) were considered truly important. Soon this interior-exterior polarity was transformed into inferior-superior polarity. The tasks performed by the female within the household, though as necessary to social life as those performed outside, were treated as inferior to the marketplace work mainly conducted by males (Sullerot, 1971:23). This ideology further accentuated the structural diminishment of a housewife's contribution, in the productive sector of the economy, consequent to mechanization. When increased mechanization transformed the family unit from a unit of production into a unit of consumption, it also made the housewife marginal to the economy. Her contribution at home was considered—

from the marketplace perspective—to be devoid of sufficient moral or psychological input justify her work as an occupation.

Yet, when we look at the extent of economic loss arising from the absence of a housewife, we can break down the average housewife's usual activities into an amalgam of anywhere from four to sixteen describable occupations. Tacitly assuming that, at the minimal level, housewives need somewhat identical skills (cooking, cleaning, budgetary regulation, housekeeping), the occupational significance of a housewife's work in marketplace terms can be ascertained by equating the cost of those of her service that are interchangeable with comparable services available in the marketplace. Chong So Pyun (1973) has estimated this cost to be slightly higher than $7,500 per year for an American housewife.

Thus, the contribution of a housewife is by no means insignificant even by the standards of marketplace exchange. We saw no reason not to treat the work of a housewife as an occupation.

(*ii*) Having decided to treat "housewife" as an occupation, we had, from among the Treiman (1975) scores, a choice of the following prestige scores that could be assigned to the occupation housewife (The prefixes represent the occupation-identification digits, while the numerals suffixed are the prestige scores): 900—Laborer; 32; 09950—Skilled Worker, 42; 0997—Semi-skilled Worker, n.e.c.: 33; 12—unclassifiable occupations: 40 and 13—Not in Labor Force: 41.

Assigning any of these specific scores to the occupation "housewife" presents a problem of equivalence and evaluation. Holding the erratic effects of supply and demand equations constant, one can safely assume that there is a positive and strong—if somewhat circuitous—relationship between an occupation's income skill, degree of autonomy and chances of mobility, and prestige scoring. Of these, the autonomy, chances for mobility and the income level of a full-time housewife are generally determined by the social placement of her husband. The tyranny of derivative status blocks out an independent interplay between these three factors. On these criteria of skill level, the inter- and intra-societal variation in skills required of a housewife to do her jobs are too wide to allow any categorization of the housewife into prestige scores available for the skilled, semi-skilled or unskilled workers. There are similar difficulties in including or excluding the occupation "housewife" for the category "Not in Labor Force." In India, where the majority of the families continue to be engaged in the primary sectors of production, it is difficult to determine when a housewife becomes or ceases to be a member of the Indian labor force. Given these limitations, we decided to categorize the occupation "housewife" in the prestige score available for unclassifiable occupations, putting a housewife's prestige rating at a score higher than that of the semi-skilled laborer but lower than the skilled laborer.

(8) The following occupations were also assigned the group score for 12-Unclassifiable Occupations: terrorist, wrestler, prostitute, magician, sorcerer, wizard, witch, imp, angel, fairy, fairy-queen, godfairy, pupil, student, devil, devil assistant and prisoner.

## Mean Prestige Scores

The male and female occupations in the sample of lessons were categorized separately by 1) Author's Sex (male, female, male & female anonymous, 2) Prescribing Agency (Central Board, Haryana, Kurukshetra, NCERT, Punjab, Rajasthan, U.P., Indeterminate), 3) Grade Level (high school, higher secondary, pre-university), 4) Lesson Type (biography, non-biography, 5) Origin (Indian, non-Indian). To make the 138 lists generated by the above classifications comparable, we calculated the Mean Prestige Score for each of these lists. The Mean Prestige Score of an occupation list was arrived at in the following manner:

The frequency of an occupation multiplied by its prestige score provided us with the salience score for an occupation in a given list. The sum of these salience scores, divided by the number of occupations in a given list, gave us the Mean Prestige score for that list.

To further validate the reliability of our score means in a given list, we also computed the Mean Prestige Score of individual lessons. While collecting data for occupation count, we had used a lesson as the basic unit. Every occupation-list is basically a compilation of occupations that appear in a set of lessons grouped according to the characteristics generated by different variable categories. To avoid generalizing on the basis of such group differences which may not be reflected in the population, we tried to estimate the probability of finding, purely by chance, substantial differences, of scores in a sample drawn from the same population. It is always possible that we might get different results from different samples because they contain different lessons *and* different lessons contain occupations with different prestige scores. Thus the variation from one sample to another might not be a group characteristic, but rather a consequence of variation from lesson to lesson.

To determine the magnitude of this lesson-to-lesson variation, we treated each lesson, rather than each occupation, as the basic unit in our analysis. The mean score for a lesson was computed by the method we used for computing the Mean Prestige Score for a given list. We added all the prestige scores of occupations in a lesson and divided it by the number of occupations in that lesson. These average scores were then subjected to a one-way analysis of variance using SPSS. The "significance level" in our results gives the probability of obtaining differences greater than or equal to the observed ones purely by chance, if the groups are equal in the underlying population.

A comparison of the Occupational List Prestige Score Based Means and Lesson Prestige Score Based Means indicated no significant differences between the two mean scores. In the six lists of male and female occupations by Hindi, English and both languages, there was never a difference of more than two points in the Total List Mean Scores of the Occupational List Based and Lesson Based Mean Scores. Out of the 138 lists of male and female occupational prestige scores, the difference between the means of any one category for two lists was exceeded by a spread of more than three points only in 2.1 per cent (N-3) cases. In all other cases, the difference between Occupational List Prestige Score Based Means and Lesson Prestige Score Based Means was never more than three points for any of the remaining 98 percent (N=135) lists. We did not consider the deviation represented in 2.1 percent cases significant enough to require detailed analysis and concluded that there was no significant difference in the two means to warrant any sophisticated difference of means tests.

The range of occupational scores for both kinds of means in all the categories (N of lists=276), also shows that most of the male occupational scores seem to cluster in the 50-60 score range. In the female scores, an overwhelming majority is concentrated in the 40-50 score range. Given this, we also found it practical to use a high-low dichotomy, with the occupation prestige score of 50 as the bisecting point.

# A List of Male and Female Occupation
# Lists by Society Type

Male occupations more likely to be found in traditional societies (N=104): adventurer, angel, archduke, archer, astrologer, bandit chief, bard, baron, beggar, blacksmith, boatman, brahman, calipha, charioteer, chiefclan, chieftain, chief tribe, chief village, cobbler, coolie, counselor to king, courtier, court jester, cowherd, creator of universe, crier, devil, devil's assistant, driver cart, driver coach, driver tonga, duke, emperor, exorcist, fakir, gladiator, God, God of death, God of death assistant, God of harvest, God of water, God of wind, guru, gypsy, harpooner, herald, hermit, hunter, imp, king's dwarf, knight, landlord, lord, magician, medicine man, messenger, miller, minister king, nawab, nobleman, officer court, official court, oilpresser, outlaw, page, peasant, peon, pharoah, pirate, prince, prophet, pupil, rickshaw driver, robber, ruffian, ruler, sadhu, sage, saint, scribe, servant, shepherd, slave, snake charmer, sorcerer, spirits of waters, squire, storyteller, street hawker, sultan, torchbearer, tradersalve, Tsar, vegetable man, warlock, warrior, washer man, weaver, wheelwright, wisemen, witch doctor, wizard, woodcutter.

Male occupations likely to be found in the industrailized societies (N=94): astronaut, bacteriologist, barrister, brigadier, broker, cabin boy, captain navy, captain submarine, chairman municipality, civil servant, clerk bank, clerk post office, collector district, colonel, conductor bus, contractor, cricketer, dean medical school, dentist, deputy collector, deputy commissioner, deputy registrar deeds, detective, driver tank, driver taxi, driver transport, editor magazine, editor newspaper, electrician, elocutionist, engineer, engineer radio, film director, flydriver, geologist, inspector school, insurance man, janitor, journalist, junk dealer, lawyer, legislator, librarian, lieutenant, lieutenant colonel, lineman, linen draper, machine gunner, major, manager, manager business, manager factory, manager of estate, mechanic air force, medical attendant, medical examiner member district board, newspaper man, officer railway, operator ship, optometrist. parachutist, parliament member, photographer, phyisologist, physiotherapist, pilot, police inspector, postal clerk, postman, postmaster, principal college, principal school, proofreader, psychiatrist, publisher, publisher printer, radio operator, railway guard, reporter, scientist, scriptwriter, secretary, secretary medical school, secretary parliament, senator, social worker, superintendent, supervisor sanitary, surgeon, typist, vice chancellor, vice president nation, waiter.

Male occupations common to both types of societies (N=193): accountant, actor, administrator, admiral, ambassador, apprentice, apprentice lawyer, archbishop, architect, artist, attendant, attendant stable, baker, band master, barber, bearer, bike builder, bishop, bodyguard, book-seller, botanist, burglar, businessman, butcher, butler, cannon loader, captain, captain ferryboat, captain ship, carpenter, carrier water, chemist, chief justice, clergyman, clerk, clerk copying, clerk court, clerk lawyer, clockmaker, clown, commander army, commander-in-chief, commander navy, commander ship, commanding officer, commissioner, confectioner, con man, cook, corporal, counselor to mayor, councilor town, courier, crew member, critic literary, curator, dispatch rider, doctor assistant, doctor medical, doctor of laws, dramatist druggist, editor, educator, elephant trainer, executioner, explorer, farmer, farmworker, fisherman forester, fruit seller, gamekeeper, gardener, gatekeeper, general, gentleman, goldsmith, governor, governor general, grocer, guard, guide, gunner, hairdresser, hatter, head clerk, headmaster, helmsman, historian, holyman, horseman, informer, innkeeper, inventor, jailor, jeweler, judge, juggler, laborer, land-valuer, leader political, leader religious, magistrate, mariner, mason, mayor, merchant, merchant tea, merchant wine, milkman, minister-chief, minister political, missionary religious, money-lender, monk, mountaineer, munshi, musician, office employee, officer, officer army, officer forest, officer revenue, officer ship, orderly, overseer, painter, painter court, philosoher, piper, planter, poet, policeman, police officer, pope, porter, potter, preacher, president nation, priest, prime minister, professor, rancher, researcher, revolutionary, sailing master, sailor, sales, agent, salesman, sarpanch, scholar, scout, sculptor, sea diver, seaman, secretary personal, secretary private, secretary to king, securtiy officer, seller perfume, sergeant, sherpa, shipmaster, shipmate, shoemaker, shop assistant, shopkeeper, silversmith, social reformer, soldier, song-writer, sportsman, spy, stonecutter, storekeeper, army, student, tailor, teacher, teacher music, terrorist, trader, tradesman, translator, traveler, valet, viceroy, watchman, waterman holy, wrestler, writer.

Female occupations likely to be found in the traditional societies (N=32) beggar, coak courtlady, duchess, fairy, fairyqueeen goddess, god fairy, governess, gypsy, holywoman, kitchen maid, lady/lord wife, maid servant, marchioness, matron, nanny, peasant, princess, prostitute, pupil, queen, queen ruler, saint, scullion seller bangle, shepherdess, slave, warrior, wahserwoman, weaver, witch.

Female occupations likely to be found in the industrialized societies (N=12): dealer hair, dietician, factory worker, governor, mathematician, minister political, pathologist, prime minister, professor, scientist, social worker, teacher deaf.

Female occupations common to both types of societies (N=28): artist, cleaning woman, commander army, dancer, deliverer milk, doctor medical, farmer, farm worker, housekeeper, housewife, laborer, landlady, leader political, milliner's apprentice, nun, nurse, poet, priest, reverend mother, scholar, seamstress, soldier, student, sweeper, teacher, teacher violin, traveller, writer.

# List of Occupations Assigned
# Only to the Male

Accountant, actor, administrator, admiral, adventurer, ambassador, apprentice lawyer, archbishop, archduke, archer, architect, astrologer, astronaut, attendant, attendant stable, bacteriologist, baker, bandit chief, band master, barber, bard, baron, barrister, bearer, bike-builder, bishop, blacksmith, boatman, bodyguard, bookseller, botanist, brahman, brigadier, broker, burglar, businessman, butcher, bulter, cabin boy, calipha, cannon loader, captain, captain ferryboat, captain navy, captain ship, captain submarine, carpenter, carrier water, chairman municipality, charioteer, chemist, chief clan, chief justice, chieftain, chief tribe, chief village, civil servant, clergyman, clerk, clerk bank, clerk copying, clerk court, clerk lawyer, clerk post office, clock-maker, clown, cobbler, collector district, colonel, commander, commander deputy, commander-in-chief, commander navy, commander ship, commanding officer, commissioner, conductor bus, confectioner, con man, contractor, coolie, corporal, counselor to king, counselor to mayor, councilor town, courier, court jester, cowherd, creator of universe, crew member, cricketer, crier, critic literary, curator, dean medical school, dentist, deputy collector, deputy commissioner, deputy registrar deeds, detective, devil, devil's assistant, dispatch rider, doctor's assistant, doctor of laws, dramatist, driver cart, driver coach, driver tank, driver taxi, driver tonga, driver transport, druggist, editor, editor magazine, editor newspaper, educator, electrician, elephant trainer, elocutionist, emperor, engineer, engineer radio, executioner, exorcist, explorer, fakir, film director, fisherman, flydriver, forester, fruit seller, gamekeeper, gardener, gatekeeper, general, gentleman, geologist, gladiator, god of death, god of death assistant, god of harvest, god of water, god of wind, goldsmith, governor-general, grocer, guard, guide, gunner, guru, hairdresser, harpooner, hatter, head clerk, headmaster, helmsman, herald, hermit, historian, horseman, hunter, imp, informer, innkeeper, inspector school, insurance man, inventor, jailor, janitor, jeweler, journalist, judge, juggler, junk dealer, king's dwarf, knight, landlord, land-valuer, lawyer, leader religious, legislator, librarian, lieutenant, lieutenant colonel, lineman, linen draper, machine-gunner, magician, magistrate, major, manager, manager business, manager factory, manager of estate, mariner, mason, mayor, mechanic air force, medical attendant, medical examiner, machine man, member district board, merchant, merchant tea, merchant wine, messenger, miller, minister chief, minister king, missionary religious, money lender, monk, mountaineer, munshi, musician, nawab, newspaper man, nobleman, office employee, officer, officer army, officer court, officer forest, officer railway, officer revenue, officer ship, official court, oil presser, operator ship, optometrist, orderly, outlaw, overseer, page, painter, painter court, parachutist, parliament member, peon, pharoah, philosopher, photographer, physiologist, pilot, piper, pirate, planter, police inspector, policeman, police officer, pope, porter, postal clerk, postman, postmaster, potter, preacher, president nation, principal college, principal school, proofreader, prophet, psychiatrist, publisher, publisher/printer, radio operator, railway guard, rancher, reporter, researcher, revolutionary, rickshaw driver, robber, ruffian, ruler, sadhu, sage, sailing master, sailor, sales agent, salesman, sarpanch, scout, scribe, script writer, sculptor, sea diver, seaman, secretary, secretary medical school, secretary parliament, secretary personal, secretary private, secretary to king, security officer, seller perfume, senator, sergeant, sherpa, shipmaster, shipmate, shoemaker, shop assistant, silversmith, snake charmer, social reformer, song writer, sorcerer, spirit of waters, sportsman, spy, squire, stone-cutter, storekeeper army, storyteller, sultan, superintendent, supervisor sanitary, surgeon, terrorist, torchbearer, trader, trader slave, tradesman, translator, tsar, typist, valet, vagetable man, vice chancellor, vice president nation, viceroy, waiter, watchman, waterman holy, wheelwright, wiseman, witch doctor, wizard, woodcutter, wrestler (N=344).

# Occupational Prestige Scores and Salience Scores for the Male and Female Characters in the PITB

## OCCUPATIONS ASSIGNED TO THE MALES

| Occupation | Prestige Score | Frequency | Salience Score |
|---|---|---|---|
| Accountant | 68 | 4 | 272 |
| Actor | 52 | 5 | 260 |
| Administrator | 64 | 10 | 640 |
| Admiral | 73 | 4 | 292 |
| Adventurer | 85 | 1 | 85 |
| Ambassador | 87 | 1 | 87 |
| Angel | 40 | 2 | 80 |
| Apprentice | 29 | 1 | 29 |
| Apprenticelawyer | 65 | 1 | 65 |
| Archbishop | 83 | 1 | 83 |
| Archduke | 64 | 1 | 64 |
| Archer | 39 | 3 | 117 |
| Architect | 72 | 4 | 288 |
| Artist | 57 | 3 | 171 |
| Astrologer | 56 | 2 | 112 |
| Astronaut | 80 | 2 | 160 |
| Attendant | 17 | 2 | 34 |
| Attendantstable | 17 | 3 | 51 |
| Bacteriologist | 79 | 1 | 79 |
| Baker | 33 | 3 | 99 |
| Bandichief | 41 | 1 | 41 |

| Occupation | Prestige Score | Frequency | Salience Score |
|---|---|---|---|
| Bandmaster | 45 | 1 | 45 |
| Barber | 30 | 7 | 210 |
| Bard | 62 | 2 | 124 |
| Baron | 64 | 2 | 128 |
| Barrister | 71 | 5 | 355 |
| Bearer | 23 | 3 | 69 |
| Beggar | 15 | 4 | 60 |
| Bikebuilder | 42 | 1 | 42 |
| Bishop | 83 | 2 | 166 |
| Blacksmith | 34 | 4 | 136 |
| Boatman | 23 | 5 | 115 |
| Bodyguard | 30 | 3 | 90 |
| Bookseller | 38 | 1 | 38 |
| Botanist | 69 | 1 | 69 |
| Brahman | 46 | 7 | 322 |
| Brigadier | 73 | 1 | 73 |
| Broker | 56 | 1 | 56 |
| Burglar | 41 | 1 | 41 |
| Businessman | 58 | 21 | 1218 |
| Butcher | 31 | 4 | 124 |
| Butler | 37 | 2 | 74 |
| Cabinboy | 17 | 1 | 17 |
| Calipha | 90 | 1 | 90 |
| Cannonloader | 42 | 1 | 42 |
| Captain | 63 | 8 | 504 |
| Captainferryboat | 63 | 1 | 63 |
| Captainnavy | 63 | 1 | 63 |
| Captainship | 63 | 5 | 315 |
| Captain submarine | 63 | 1 | 63 |
| Carpenter | 37 | 9 | 333 |
| Carrierwater | 17 | 3 | 51 |
| Chairman municipality | 68 | 2 | 136 |
| Charioteer | 42 | 3 | 126 |
| Chemist | 69 | 2 | 138 |
| Chiefclan | 63 | 1 | 63 |
| Chief justice | 82 | 3 | 246 |
| Chieftain | 63 | 6 | 378 |

| Occupation | Prestige Score | Frequency | Salience Score |
|---|---|---|---|
| Chief tribe | 63 | 2 | 126 |
| Chiefvillage | 42 | 3 | 147 |
| Civilservant | 55 | 4 | 220 |
| Clergyman | 60 | 6 | 360 |
| Clerk | 41 | 7 | 287 |
| Clerkbank | 41 | 1 | 41 |
| Clerkcopying | 41 | 1 | 41 |
| Clerkcourt | 41 | 2 | 82 |
| Clerklawyer | 41 | 4 | 164 |
| Clerkpostoffice | 39 | 1 | 39 |
| Clockmaker | 40 | 1 | 40 |
| Clown | 33 | 1 | 33 |
| Cobbler | 28 | 1 | 28 |
| Collectordistrict | 66 | 1 | 66 |
| Colonel | 63 | 2 | 126 |
| Commander | 73 | 4 | 292 |
| Commander army | 73 | 6 | 438 |
| Commander deputy | 63 | 1 | 63 |
| Commander-in-chief | 73 | 7 | 511 |
| Commander navy | 73 | 1 | 73 |
| Commandership | 63 | 1 | 63 |
| Commanding officer | 63 | 2 | 126 |
| Commissioner | 82 | 1 | 82 |
| Conductorbus | 26 | 2 | 52 |
| Confectioner | 33 | 4 | 132 |
| Conman | 41 | 2 | 82 |
| Contractor | 49 | 3 | 147 |
| Cook | 31 | 11 | 341 |
| Coolie | 14 | 5 | 70 |
| Corporal | 44 | 2 | 88 |
| Councillortoking | 50 | 1 | 50 |
| Councillortomayor | 50 | 1 | 50 |
| Councillortown | 55 | 1 | 55 |
| Courier | 26 | 1 | 26 |
| Courtier | 41 | 10 | 410 |
| Courtjester | 33 | 3 | 99 |
| Cowherd | 26 | 1 | 26 |

| Occupation | Prestige Score | Frequency | Salience Score |
|---|---|---|---|
| Creatorofuniverse | 85 | 1 | 85 |
| Crewmember | 29 | 2 | 58 |
| Crickter | 48 | 1 | 48 |
| Crier | 26 | 1 | 26 |
| Critic literary | 62 | 4 | 248 |
| Curator | 54 | 1 | 54 |
| Deanmedicalschool | 86 | 1 | 86 |
| Dentist | 70 | 1 | 70 |
| Deputycollector | 66 | 2 | 132 |
| Deputycommissioner | 66 | 1 | 66 |
| Deputyregistrardeeds | 66 | 1 | 66 |
| Detective | 48 | 3 | 144 |
| Devil | 40 | 2 | 80 |
| Devilassistant | 40 | 1 | 40 |
| Dispatchrider | 33 | 1 | 33 |
| Doctorasst | 50 | 2 | 100 |
| Doctormedical | 78 | 42 | 3276 |
| Doctoroflaws | 78 | 1 | 78 |
| Dramatist | 62 | 7 | 434 |
| Drivercart | 26 | 3 | 78 |
| Drivercoach | 26 | 6 | 156 |
| Drivertank | 39 | 1 | 39 |
| Drivertaxi | 28 | 3 | 84 |
| Drivertonga | 26 | 2 | 52 |
| Drivertransport | 39 | 2 | 78 |
| Druggist | 64 | 1 | 64 |
| Duke | 64 | 5 | 320 |
| Editor | 56 | 6 | 336 |
| Editormagazine | 56 | 1 | 56 |
| Editornewspaper | 65 | 3 | 195 |
| Educator | 61 | 4 | 244 |
| Electrician | 44 | 1 | 44 |
| Elephanttrainer | 42 | 1 | 42 |
| Elocutionist | 62 | 1 | 62 |
| Emperor | 90 | 19 | 1710 |
| Engineer | 58 | 10 | 580 |
| Engineerradio | 65 | 1 | 65 |

| Occupation | Prestige Score | Frequency | Salience Score |
|---|---|---|---|
| Executioner | 42 | 1 | 42 |
| Exorcist | 22 | 1 | 22 |
| Explorer | 49 | 6 | 294 |
| Fakir | 56 | 1 | 56 |
| Farmer | 47 | 28 | 1316 |
| Farmworker | 23 | 5 | 115 |
| Filmdirector | 62 | 1 | 62 |
| Fisherman | 28 | 13 | 364 |
| Flydriver | 42 | 1 | 42 |
| Forester | 48 | 1 | 48 |
| Fruitseller | 22 | 3 | 66 |
| Gamekeeper | 48 | 1 | 48 |
| Gardener | 21 | 7 | 147 |
| Gatekeeper | 22 | 7 | 154 |
| General | 73 | 12 | 876 |
| Gentleman | 41 | 6 | 246 |
| Geologist | 67 | 1 | 67 |
| Gladiator | 17 | 1 | 17 |
| God | 85 | 8 | 680 |
| Godofdeath | 64 | 3 | 192 |
| Godofdeathasst | 54 | 1 | 54 |
| Godofharvest | 64 | 1 | 64 |
| Godofwater | 64 | 1 | 64 |
| Godwind | 64 | 1 | 64 |
| Goldsmith | 43 | 3 | 129 |
| Governor | 82 | 8 | 656 |
| Governor-general | 90 | 1 | 90 |
| Grocer | 42 | 5 | 210 |
| Guard | 30 | 9 | 270 |
| Guide | 29 | 9 | 261 |
| Gunner | 42 | 1 | 42 |
| Guru | 62 | 6 | 372 |
| Gypsy | 40 | 1 | 40 |
| Hairdresser | 35 | 1 | 35 |
| Harpooner | 40 | 1 | 40 |
| Hatter | 32 | 1 | 32 |
| Headclerk | 54 | 3 | 162 |

| Occupation | Prestige Score | Frequeney | Salience Score |
|---|---|---|---|
| Headmaster | 66 | 8 | 528 |
| Helmsman | 23 | 1 | 23 |
| Herald | 26 | 1 | 26 |
| Hermit | 56 | 2 | 112 |
| Historian | 67 | 4 | 268 |
| Holyman | 56 | 7 | 392 |
| Horseman | 39 | 6 | 234 |
| Hunter | 6 | 4 | 24 |
| Imp | 40 | 1 | 40 |
| Informer | 54 | 1 | 54 |
| Inkkeeper | 37 | 5 | 185 |
| Inspector school | 68 | 1 | 68 |
| Insurance man | 44 | 1 | 44 |
| Inventor | 85 | 7 | 595 |
| Jailor | 52 | 4 | 208 |
| Janitor | 21 | 1 | 21 |
| Jeweller | 43 | 1 | 43 |
| Journalist | 55 | 6 | 330 |
| Judge | 78 | 15 | 1170 |
| Juggler | 33 | 3 | 99 |
| Junk dealer | 42 | 1 | 42 |
| King | 90 | 89 | 8010 |
| Kings dwarf | 33 | 1 | 33 |
| Knight | 64 | 6 | 384 |
| Labourer | 32 | 15 | 480 |
| Landlord | 65 | 14 | 910 |
| Landvaluer | 54 | 1 | 54 |
| Lawyer | 71 | 27 | 1917 |
| Leaderpolitical | 85 | 19 | 1615 |
| Leaderreligious | 85 | 5 | 425 |
| Legislator | 64 | 2 | 128 |
| Librarian | 54 | 1 | 54 |
| Lieutenant | 63 | 4 | 252 |
| Lieutenant colonel | 63 | 1 | 63 |
| Lineman | 36 | 1 | 36 |
| Linen draper | 40 | 1 | 40 |
| Lord | 64 | 8 | 512 |

| Occupation | Prestige Score | Frequency | Salience Score |
|---|---|---|---|
| Machinegunner | 42 | 1 | 42 |
| Magician | 40 | 3 | 120 |
| Magistrate | 73 | 8 | 584 |
| Major | 63 | 3 | 189 |
| Manager | 63 | 4 | 252 |
| Managerbusiness | 67 | 1 | 67 |
| Managerfactory | 61 | 1 | 61 |
| Managerofestate | 65 | 2 | 130 |
| Mariner | 35 | 1 | 35 |
| Mason | 34 | 1 | 34 |
| Mayor | 68 | 7 | 476 |
| Mechanicalforce | 42 | 1 | 42 |
| Medicalattendant | 42 | 1 | 42 |
| Medicalexaminer | 78 | 1 | 78 |
| Medicineman | 29 | 1 | 29 |
| Member district board | 55 | 1 | 55 |
| Merchant | 48 | 12 | 576 |
| Merchanttea | 48 | 1 | 48 |
| Merchantwine | 48 | 1 | 48 |
| Messenger | 26 | 10 | 260 |
| Milkman | 24 | 3 | 72 |
| Miller | 42 | 4 | 168 |
| Ministerchief | 82 | 2 | 164 |
| Ministerking | 79 | 5 | 395 |
| Minister political | 79 | 18 | 1422 |
| Missionaryreligious | 49 | 3 | 147 |
| Moneylender | 15 | 11 | 165 |
| Monk | 56 | 9 | 504 |
| Mountaineer | 48 | 5 | 240 |
| Munshi | 48 | 1 | 49 |
| Musician | 56 | 5 | 280 |
| Nawab | 82 | 2 | 164 |
| Newspaperman | 55 | 1 | 55 |
| Nobleman | 64 | 5 | 320 |
| Officeemployee | 41 | 7 | 287 |
| Officer | 66 | 7 | 462 |
| Officerarmy | 63 | 11 | 693 |

| Occupation | Prestige Score | Frequency | Salience Score |
|---|---|---|---|
| Officercourt | 63 | 1 | 63 |
| Officerforest | 63 | 1 | 63 |
| Officerrailway | 66 | 1 | 66 |
| Officerrevenue | 52 | 3 | 156 |
| Officership | 63 | 1 | 63 |
| Officialcourt | 66 | 2 | 132 |
| Oilpresser | 42 | 1 | 42 |
| Operatorship | 42 | 1 | 42 |
| Optometrist | 62 | 1 | 62 |
| Orderly | 17 | 2 | 34 |
| Outlaw | 41 | 1 | 41 |
| Overseer | 54 | 3 | 162 |
| Page | 17 | 1 | 17 |
| Painter | 57 | 1 | 57 |
| Paintercourt | 57 | 1 | 57 |
| Parachutist | 42 | 1 | 42 |
| Parliamentmember | 72 | 2 | 144 |
| Peasant | 32 | 9 | 288 |
| Peon | 26 | 7 | 182 |
| Pharoah | 90 | 1 | 90 |
| Philosopher | 68 | 10 | 680 |
| Photographer | 45 | 3 | 135 |
| Physiologist | 78 | 1 | 78 |
| Physiotherapist | 50 | 1 | 50 |
| Pilot | 66 | 3 | 198 |
| Piper | 32 | 1 | 32 |
| Pirate | 41 | 4 | 164 |
| Planter | 63 | 1 | 63 |
| Poet | 62 | 30 | 1860 |
| Policeinspector | 60 | 4 | 240 |
| Policeman | 40 | 14 | 560 |
| Policeofficer | 60 | 9 | 540 |
| Pope | 83 | 2 | 166 |
| Porter | 17 | 4 | 68 |
| Postal clerk | 39 | 1 | 39 |
| Postman | 33 | 3 | 99 |
| Postmaster | 58 | 4 | 232 |

| *Occupation* | *Prestige Score* | *Frequency* | *Salience Score* |
|---|---|---|---|
| Potter | 25 | 1 | 25 |
| Preacher | 60 | 2 | 120 |
| Presidentnation | 90 | 9 | 810 |
| Priest | 60 | 27 | 1620 |
| Primeminister | 86 | 11 | 946 |
| Prince | 64 | 36 | 2304 |
| Principalcollege | 72 | 3 | 216 |
| Principalschool | 72 | 1 | 72 |
| Professor | 78 | 12 | 936 |
| Proofreader | 41 | 1 | 41 |
| Prophet | 85 | 6 | 510 |
| Psychiatrist | 78 | 1 | 78 |
| Publisher | 58 | 1 | 58 |
| Publisherprinter | 58 | 1 | 58 |
| Pupil | 40 | 4 | 160 |
| Radiooperator | 49 | 1 | 49 |
| Railwayguard | 39 | 3 | 117 |
| Rancher | 63 | 1 | 63 |
| Reporter | 55 | 1 | 55 |
| Researcher | 57 | 2 | 114 |
| Revolutionary | 85 | 3 | 255 |
| Rickshawdriver | 17 | 2 | 34 |
| Robber | 41 | 3 | 123 |
| Ruffian | 41 | 1 | 41 |
| Ruler | 90 | 4 | 360 |
| Sadhu | 56 | 1 | 56 |
| Sage | 56 | 4 | 224 |
| Sailingmaster | 63 | 1 | 63 |
| Sailor | 35 | 17 | 595 |
| Saint | 85 | 6 | 510 |
| Salesagent | 46 | 1 | 46 |
| Salesman | 34 | 1 | 34 |
| Sarpanch | 42 | 1 | 42 |
| Scholar | 68 | 7 | 476 |
| Scientist | 78 | 19 | 1482 |
| Scout | 49 | 1 | 49 |
| Scribe | 41 | 1 | 41 |

| Occupation | Prestige Score | Frequency | Salience Score |
|---|---|---|---|
| Scriptwriter | 56 | 1 | 56 |
| Sculptor | 51 | 1 | 51 |
| Seadiver | 35 | 1 | 35 |
| Seaman | 35 | 7 | 245 |
| Secretary | 53 | 2 | 106 |
| Secretarymedschool | 71 | 1 | 71 |
| Secretaryparliament | 71 | 1 | 71 |
| Secretarypersonal | 53 | 1 | 53 |
| Secretaryprivate | 53 | 1 | 53 |
| Secretarytoking | 71 | 1 | 71 |
| Securityofficer | 52 | 1 | 52 |
| Sellerperfume | 47 | 1 | 47 |
| Senator | 85 | 1 | 85 |
| Sergeant | 60 | 5 | 300 |
| Servant | 17 | 44 | 748 |
| Shepherd | 26 | 8 | 208 |
| Sherpa | 48 | 1 | 48 |
| Shipmaster | 63 | 2 | 126 |
| Shipmate | 35 | 1 | 35 |
| Shoemaker | 28 | 3 | 84 |
| Shopassistant | 32 | 1 | 32 |
| Shopkeeper | 42 | 11 | 462 |
| Silversmith | 43 | 2 | 86 |
| Slave | 17 | 11 | 187 |
| Shakecharmer | 33 | 1 | 33 |
| Socialreformer | 85 | 4 | 340 |
| Socialworker | 56 | 1 | 56 |
| Soldier | 39 | 52 | 2028 |
| Songwriter | 56 | 1 | 56 |
| Sorcerer | 40 | 1 | 40 |
| Spiritofwaters | 64 | 2 | 128 |
| Sportsman | 48 | 2 | 96 |
| Spy | 64 | 4 | 256 |
| Squire | 41 | 2 | 82 |
| Stonecutter | 38 | 2 | 76 |
| Storekeeperarmy | 54 | 1 | 54 |
| Storyteller | 33 | 2 | 66 |

| Occupation | Prestige Score | Frequency | Salience Score |
|---|---|---|---|
| Streethawker | 22 | 3 | 66 |
| Student | 40 | 43 | 1720 |
| Sultan | 90 | 1 | 90 |
| Superintendent | 66 | 1 | 66 |
| Supervisorsanitary | 48 | 1 | 48 |
| Surgeon | 78 | 4 | 312 |
| Tailor | 40 | 6 | 240 |
| Teacher | 61 | 42 | 2562 |
| Teachermusic | 53 | 1 | 53 |
| Terrorist | 40 | 2 | 80 |
| Torchbearer | 32 | 1 | 32 |
| Trader | 48 | 9 | 432 |
| Traderslave | 48 | 1 | 48 |
| Tradesman | 22 | 3 | 66 |
| Translator | 54 | 3 | 162 |
| Traveller | 41 | 13 | 533 |
| Tsar | 90 | 1 | 90 |
| Typist | 42 | 2 | 84 |
| Valet | 37 | 1 | 37 |
| Vegetableman | 22 | 1 | 22 |
| Vicechancellor | 86 | 1 | 86 |
| Vicepresidentnation | 82 | 1 | 82 |
| Viceroy | 90 | 4 | 360 |
| Waiter | 23 | 2 | 46 |
| Warlock | 73 | 1 | 73 |
| Warrior | 73 | 12 | 876 |
| Washerman | 22 | 8 | 176 |
| Watchman | 22 | 8 | 176 |
| Watermanholy | 46 | 1 | 46 |
| Weaver | 30 | 3 | 90 |
| Wheelwright | 42 | 1 | 42 |
| Wiseman | 68 | 2 | 136 |
| Witch doctor | 29 | 1 | 29 |
| Wizard | 40 | 1 | 40 |
| Woodcutter | 19 | 2 | 38 |
| Wrestler | 40 | 1 | 40 |
| Writer | 62 | 28 | 1736 |

Number of Occupations= 391
The Total Saliency is 1761
The Mean Score is 54.8

## OCCUPATIONS ASSIGNED TO THE *FEMALES*

| Occupation | Prestige Score | Frequency | Salience Score |
|---|---|---|---|
| Artist | 57 | 1 | 57 |
| Beggar | 15 | 1 | 15 |
| Cleaningwoman | 17 | 1 | 17 |
| Commanderarmy | 73 | 1 | 73 |
| Cook | 31 | 3 | 93 |
| Courtlady | 41 | 1 | 41 |
| Dancer | 45 | 1 | 45 |
| Dealerhair | 42 | 1 | 42 |
| Deliverer milk | 24 | 1 | 24 |
| Dietician | 52 | 1 | 52 |
| Doctormedical | 78 | 1 | 78 |
| Duchess | 64 | 1 | 64 |
| Factoryworker | 18 | 1 | 18 |
| Fairy | 40 | 1 | 40 |
| Fairyqueen | 40 | 1 | 40 |
| Farmer | 47 | 4 | 188 |
| Farmworker | 23 | 1 | 23 |
| Goddess | 64 | 4 | 256 |
| Godfairy | 40 | 1 | 40 |
| Governess | 23 | 1 | 23 |
| Governor | 82 | 1 | 82 |
| Gypsy | 41 | 1 | 41 |
| Holywoman | 56 | 2 | 112 |
| Housekeeper | 28 | 2 | 56 |
| Housewife | 40 | 118 | 4720 |
| Kitchenmaid | 25 | 2 | 50 |
| Laborer | 32 | 3 | 96 |
| Ladylordwife | 64 | 2 | 128 |
| Landlady | 57 | 1 | 57 |
| Leaderpolitical | 85 | 6 | 510 |

| *Occupation* | *Prestige Score* | *Frequency* | *Salience Score* |
|---|---|---|---|
| Maidservant | 17 | 27 | 459 |
| Marchioness | 64 | 1 | 64 |
| Mathematician | 69 | 1 | 69 |
| Matron | 17 | 1 | 17 |
| Millinersapprentice | 32 | 1 | 32 |
| Ministerpolitical | 79 | 1 | 79 |
| Nanny | 23 | 2 | 46 |
| Nun | 58 | 2 | 112 |
| Nurse | 54 | 11 | 594 |
| Pathologist | 78 | 1 | 78 |
| Peasant | 32 | 2 | 64 |
| Poet | 52 | 3 | 186 |
| Priest | 60 | 1 | 60 |
| Primeminister | 86 | 1 | 86 |
| Princess | 64 | 24 | 1536 |
| Professor | 78 | 1 | 78 |
| Prostitute | 40 | 2 | 80 |
| Pupil | 40 | 1 | 40 |
| Queen | 64 | 30 | 1920 |
| Queenruler | 90 | 3 | 270 |
| Reverendmother | 83 | 1 | 83 |
| Saint | 85 | 1 | 85 |
| Scholar | 68 | 1 | 68 |
| Scientist | 78 | 1 | 78 |
| Scullion | 25 | 1 | 25 |
| Seamstress | 39 | 1 | 39 |
| Sellerbangle | 22 | 1 | 22 |
| Shepherdess | 26 | 1 | 26 |
| Slave | 17 | 1 | 17 |
| Socialworker | 56 | 1 | 56 |
| Soldier | 39 | 1 | 39 |
| Student | 40 | 8 | 320 |
| Sweeper | 13 | 1 | 26 |
| Teacher | 61 | 3 | 183 |
| Teacherdeaf | 62 | 1 | 62 |
| Teacherviolin | 53 | 2 | 106 |
| Traveler | 41 | 1 | 41 |

| Occupation | Prestige Score | Frequency | Salience Score |
|---|---|---|---|
| Warrior | 44 | 1 | 44 |
| Washerwoman | 22 | 1 | 22 |
| Weaver | 30 | 1 | 30 |
| Witch | 40 | 4 | 160 |
| Writer | 62 | 3 | 186 |

Number of Occupations =     72
The Total Saliency is       320
The Mean Score is        45.8

# SIX LISTS, COMPARISON OF MEANS:
## Occupational List—Prestige Score Based Means, Lesson Prestige Score Based Means, All Categories

## MALE, HINDI LANGUAGE

| | | | |
|---|---|---|---|
| | List Mean Score | Mean=56.5 | 54.5 |
| Author Sex | Male | Mean=57.0 | 54.6 |
| Author Sex | Female | Mean=43.6 | 41.9 |
| Author Sex | Both | Mean=00.0 | |
| Author Sex | Anonymous | Mean=56.4 | 54.5 |
| Author Sex | Indeterminate | Mean=00.0 | |
| Agency | Central Board | Mean=50.3 | 50.0 |
| Agency | Haryana | Mean=55.0 | 54.3 |
| Agency | Kurukshetra | Mean=59.8 | 57.7 |
| Agency | NCERT | Mean=55.2 | 56.3 |
| Agency | Punjab | Mean=50.4 | 49.2 |
| Agency | Rajasthan | Mean=59.8 | 57.0 |
| Agency | U.P. | Mean=54.1 | 53.3 |
| Agency | Indeterminate | Mean=00.0 | |
| Grade | High School | Mean=51.8 | 50.8 |
| Grade | Higher Secondary | Mean=57.7 | 55.7 |
| Grade | Pre-University | Mean=59.8 | 57.7 |
| Grade | Other | Mean=00.0 | |
| Grade | Indeterminate | Mean=00.0 | |
| Lesson Type | Biography | Mean=62.4 | 62.5 |
| Lesson Type | Non-Biography | Mean=52.6 | 50.9 |
| Origin | Indian | Mean=56.8 | 54.6 |

Origin              Non-Indian          Mean=54.3          53.8

## MALE, BOTH LANGUAGES

|              |                   |            |       |
|--------------|-------------------|------------|-------|
|              | List Mean Score   | Mean=54.8  | 53.4  |
| Author Sex   | Male              | Mean=55.0  | 53.4  |
| Author Sex   | Female            | Mean=54.1  | 51.7  |
| Author Sex   | Both              | Mean=47.1  | 47.2  |
| Author Sex   | Anonymous         | Mean=54.8  | 54.2  |
| Author Sex   | Indeterminate     | Mean=00.0  |       |
| Agency       | Central Board     | Mean=51.5  | 50.5  |
| Agency       | Haryana           | Mean=60.2  | 60.8  |
| Agency       | Kurukshetra       | Mean=56.7  | 53.1  |
| Agency       | NCERT             | Mean=55.9  | 55.8  |
| Agency       | Punjab            | Mean=48.4  | 48.3  |
| Agency       | Rajasthan         | Mean=56.2  | 54.4  |
| Agency       | U.P.              | Mean=54.3  | 53.8  |
| Agency       | Indeterminate     | Mean=00.0  |       |
| Grade        | High School       | Mean=52.7  | 51.8  |
| Grade        | Higher Secondary  | Mean=56.7  | 55.1  |
| Grade        | Pre-University    | Mean=56.7  | 53.1  |
| Grade        | Other             | Mean=00 0  |       |
| Grade        | Indeterminate     | Mean=00.0  |       |
| Lesson Type  | Biography         | Mean=60.7  | 59.5  |
| Lesson Type  | Non-Biography     | Mean=52.3  | 50.9  |
| Origin       | Indian            | Mean=55.9  | 54.6  |
| Origin       | Non-Indian        | Mean=53.3  | 51.8  |

## FEMALE, HINDI LANGUAGE

|              |                   |            |       |
|--------------|-------------------|------------|-------|
|              | List Mean Score   | Mean=42.2  | 41.3  |
| Author Sex   | Male              | Mean=42.0  | 41.2  |
| Author Sex   | Female            | Mean=43.2  | 42.5  |
| Author Sex   | Both              | Mean=00.0  |       |
| Author Sex   | Anonymous         | Mean=00.0  |       |
| Agency       | Central Board     | Mean=39.7  | 44.3  |
| Agency       | Haryana           | Mean=34.2  | 36.1  |
| Agency       | Kurukshetra       | Mean=44.3  | 46.4  |

| Agency | NCERT | Mean=33.5 | 32.0 |
|---|---|---|---|
| Agency | Punjab | Mean=32.0 | 31.3 |
| Agency | Rajasthan | Mean=46.0 | 43.2 |
| Agency | U.P. | Mean=42.4 | 40.5 |
| Grade | High School | Mean=35.6 | 34.5 |
| Grade | Higher Secondary | Mean=43.4 | 42.2 |
| Grade | Pre-University | Mean=44.3 | 46.4 |
| Grade | Other | Mean=00.0 | |
| Lesson Type | Biography | Mean=49.6 | 46.3 |
| Lesson Type | Non-Biography | Mean=38.6 | 39.2 |
| Origin | Indian | Mean=42.4 | 41.9 |
| Origin | Non-Indian | Mean=38.0 | 35.3 |

## FEMALE, ENGLISH LANGUAGE

| | List Mean Score | Mean=48.3 | 46.6 |
|---|---|---|---|
| Author Sex | Male | Mean=47.0 | 45.1 |
| Author Sex | Female | Mean=49.9 | 49.3 |
| Author Sex | Both | Mean=40.0 | 40.0 |
| Author Sex | Anonymous | Mean=53.0 | 50.3 |
| Agency | Central Board | Mean=44.5 | 41.3 |
| Agency | Haryana | Mean=67.5 | 66.5 |
| Agency | Kurukshetra | Mean=48.0 | 45.8 |
| Agency | NCERT | Mean=47.3 | 47.9 |
| Agency | Punjab | Mean=43.1 | 43.8 |
| Agency | Rajasthan | Mean=51.6 | 50.2 |
| Agency | U.P. | Mean=47.9 | 47.9 |
| Grade | High School | Mean=48.7 | 47.8 |
| Grade | Higher Secondary | Mean=47.9 | 46.4 |
| Grade | Pre-University | Mean=48.0 | 45.8 |
| Grade | Other | Mean=00.0 | |
| Lesson Type | Biography | Mean=54.9 | 53.9 |
| Lesson Type | Non-Biography | Mean=46.8 | 45.8 |
| Origin | Indian | Mean=53.5 | 51.1 |
| Origin | Non-Indian | Mean=44.2 | 43.6 |

## FEMALE, BOTH LANGUAGES

| | List Mean Score | Mean=45.8 | 44.3 |
|---|---|---|---|
| Author Sex | Male | Mean=44.4 | 43.1 |

| | | | |
|---|---|---|---|
| Author Sex | Female | Mean=48.7 | 47.7 |
| Author Sex | Both | Mean=40.0 | 40.0 |
| Author Sex | Anonymous | Mean=53.0 | 50.3 |
| Agency | Central Board | Mean=42.9 | 42.1 |
| Agency | Haryana | Mean=55.4 | 51.3 |
| Agency | Kurukshetra | Mean=46.3 | 46.2 |
| Agency | NCERT | Mean=41.8 | 40.5 |
| Agency | Punjab | Mean=38.2 | 37.9 |
| Agency | Rajasthan | Mean=48.3 | 46.3 |
| Agency | U.P. | Mean=47.0 | 46.6 |
| Grade | High School | Mean=46.1 | 45.2 |
| Grade | Higher Secondary | Mean=45.5 | 44.0 |
| Grade | Pre-University | Mean=46.3 | 46.2 |
| Grade | Other | Mean=00.0 | |
| Lesson Type | Biography | Mean=52.2 | 49.7 |
| Lesson Type | Non-Biography | Mean=43.8 | 43 2 |
| Origin | Indian | Mean=47.1 | 45.7 |
| Origin | Non-Indian | Mean=43.5 | 42.6 |

# List of Textbooks, Arranged by Text ID Numbers

Text I.D.

01. Pant, H.C. and Vyas, S.S. eds. No date. Glorious Tales (Prescribed English text for class IX in Rajasthan). Jaipur: Rajasthan Prakashan.

02. Bhandari, C.S. and Ram, S.K. 1975. The Framework of English (Prescribed for XI class by the Board of Secondary Education, Rajasthan). Ajmer: Misra Brothers.

03. Rust, J.C.W., Srivastava, B.D. and McFarland, D.E. 1974. Olympic English Course Reader (Prescribed English text for class X in Rajasthan). Madras: Macmillan Co. of India Ltd.

04. Prashad, B. 1975. A Book of Golden Tales (Prescribed English text for higher secondary classes, Rajasthan). Agra: Sri Ram Mehra & Co.

05. Rust, J.C.W., Srivastava, B.D. and McFarland, D.E. eds. 1975 (Revised Edition). Olympic English Course Reader (For class IX in Rajasthan). Madras: The Macmillan Co. of India Ltd.

06. Aggarwal, S., ed. 1975. Ekanki Sangrah (Prescribed Hindi text for secondary examination, Rajasthan Board). Chandausi: G.R. Bhargav & Sons.

07. Chaturvedi, N. and Bijawat, K.G., eds. 1974. Uchh-Madh-yamic Gadya-Padya-Sangrah (Prescribed compulsory Hindi text for class XI Rajasthan). Jaipur: Rajasthan Prakashan.

08. Rustogi, K.G., ed. 1975. Path Praneta (Prescribed for higher secondary classes IX and X in Rajasthan). Delhi:

Frank Brothers & Co.

09. Marwa, K., ed. 1974. Kahaani-Sangarh (Prescribed for higher secondary examination in compulsory Hindi, Rajasthan). Ajmer: Raavat Pustak Bhandar.

10. Shrishrimal, S., ed. 1974. Katha Prasoon (Prescribed Hindi text for higher secondary examination in Rajasthan). Chandausi: G.R. Bhargav & Sons.

11. Vajpayee, V. and Sharma, R.C., eds. 1974. Madhyamic Gadya-Padya-Sangrah (Prescribed compulsory Hindi text for secondary students). Agra: Vishnu Prakashan.

12. Chaturvedi, B.L., ed. 1975. Parimal (For IX and X class). New Delhi: Central Board of Secondary Education.

13. Gupta, S.C., ed. 1975. Lalit Sankalan (For IX and X class). New Delhi: Central Board of Secondary Education.

14. Joshi, G.D. 1975. Saras Bharati (Collection of articles, text for higher secondary classes). New Delhi: Central Board of Secondary Education.

15. Central Institute of English and Foreign Languages, Hyderabad. 1975. An English Course for Secondary Schools, Part I (For class IX). New Delhi: Central Board of Secondary Education.

16. Bagchi, G. and Nag, B., eds. 1975. English Prose and Poetry Selections. New Delhi: Central Board of Secondary Education.

17. Mehrotra, P.V., ed. 1975 English Rapid Reader. New Delhi: Central Board of Secondary Education.

18. Collocott, T.C., ed. 1974, 18th Printing. New Radiant Readers Book IX (English text for standard IX in English medium schools. Prescribed for schools in U.P. and Maharashtra). New Delhi: Allied Publishers Private Ltd.

19. Collocott, T.C.. ed. 1974 (Revised and Enlarged Edition). New Radiant Readers Book VIII (Standard VIII of English medium schools in U.P. and Maharashtra). New Delhi: Allied Publishers.

20. Aggarwala, N.K., ed. 1974. Footprints of the Great (Prescribed for higher secondary and intermediate classes in U.P.). Agra: Ram Prasad & Sons.

21. Singh, B., ed. 1972 (1969, 1968). Indra Dhanush (Hindi text for English medium schools in U.P.). New Delhi:

Hemkunt Press.

22. Urling-Smith, F.M. 1971 (1951, 1937). Stories of Sindbad the Sailor (Retold by F.M. Urling-Smith). Madras: Oxford University Press (Indian Branch).

23. Bhandari, C.S., Spencer, J.W. and Ram, S.K. 1974 (1971, 1967, 1965, 1963, 1960, 1959, and 1958). Read and Tell, Book Seven (Prescribed text in English language for some high schools in U.P.). Calcutta: Orient Longmans Ltd.

24. Bhandari, C.S., Spencer, J.W. and Ram S.K., eds. 1966 (1964, 1958). Read and Tell Book Eight (English text for some high schools in U.P.). Calcutta: Orient Longmans Ltd.

25. Singh, U.B. 1974 (Reprint). Jeevan Aur Sahitya (Hindi text for U.P. higher secondary and intermediate classes). Agra: Shri Ram Mehra & Co.

26. Central Institute of English, Hyderabad. 1974 (1973, 1971, 1970). English Reader Book IV (For class IX, special series). New Delhi: National Council of Educational Research and Training.

27. Ojha, D. and Singh, B., eds. 1973 (1971, 1970, 1969, 1968, 1967). Ekanki Sankalan (Collection of Hindi plays, text for higher secondary classes). New Delhi: National Council of Educational Research and Training.

28. Sinha, S. and Gupta, S.C., eds. 1973 (1971, 1970, 1969, 1968). Kahani Sankalan (Hindi stories, text for higher secondary classes). New Delhi: National Council of Educational Research and Training.

29. National Council of Educational Research and Training. 1974 (1973). Gadya Bharati (Collection of articles, text for higher secondary classes). New Delhi: National Council of Educational Research and Training.

30. Central Institute of English, Hyderabad. 1973. English Reader Book VI (For class XI, special series). New Delhi: National Council of Educational Research and Training.

31. Jyoti, D.D., ed. 1974 (1973, 1972, 1971). A Book of Short Stories (Prescribed English text for matric classes in Punjab). Chandigarh: Board of School Education, Punjab.

32. Maini, D.P. and Nistandra, H.C. 1973 (1972, 1971). Charitra Aur Chintan (For Punjab matric and higher secondary, Part I). Chandigarh: Board of School Education, Punjab.

33. Bali, I. and Talwar, K.L., eds. 1974 (1973, 1972, 1971). Kuch Ekanki, Kuch Kahaaniyan (Prescribed Hindi text for matric classes in Punjab). Chandigarh: Board of School Education, Punjab.

34. Board of School, Haryana. 1975 (1974). Gadhya-Sorabh (Prescribed Hindi texts for high and higher secondary schools, Haryana). Chandigarh: Board of Schools Education, Haryana.

35. Central Institute of English, Hyderabad. 1972 (1971). English Reader Book V (For class X special series). New Delhi: National Council of Educational Research and Training.

36. Board of School Education, Haryana. 1971. A Textbook of English Prose (Prescribed for matric and higher secondary Part I examinations, Haryana). Chandigarh: Board of School Education, Haryana.

37. Eliot, G. 1974 (1934). The Mill On the Floss (Prescribed English text for the pre-university students, Kurukshetra University). New Delhi: Orient Longman Ltd.

38. Central Institute of English, Hyderabad. 1974 (1967, Tenth printing). Language Through Literature (Prescribed English Text for preparatory students of Kurukshetra University). Delhi: Oxford University Press.

39. Mackin, R., ed. 1974. Stories of Modern Adventure: Harrap's World Ahead Series (Prescribed English text for preparatory students of Kurukshetra University). Delhi: Oxford University Press.

40. Gupta, P., ed. 1974. Gadya Vividha (Prescribed Hindi text for pre-university students, Kurukshetra University). Delhi: Rajpal and Sons.

41. Sharma, L., ed. No date. Mandaakini (compulsory Hindi text for the pre-university students, Kurukshetra University). Gwalior: Kailash Pustak Sadan.

# A Review of Research on
# Sexism in Textbooks

Sex role socialization begins at an early stage when society assigns different activities, attitudes and aspirations to males and females. The content of sex roles in a given culture is derived from the prevalent definitions of reality, which are determined by the dominant ideology. Classroom practices, curriculum; attitudes of teachers and the content of textbooks all reinforce sex sterotypes. Since school-education also transmits sex role ideals, the amount of sex role stereotyping in instructional literature can indicate a society's movement toward detraditionalization.

Most of the research on sexism in textbooks has been conducted in North America. We did hear of an Indian study, reportedly financed by the National Council of Educational Research and Training, titled "Women and Girls as Portrayed in the English language Textbooks, Published by the Central Institute of English, Hyderabad." We wrote to the Director of NCERT requesting for a copy. In this reply dated December 8, 1976, Professor R. P. Singh informed us that the report had been sent to experts for assessment, and, "NCERT will have a final decision about its publication on receipt of the expert advice."

The following review is based on research conducted on countries other than India. In the earlier half of the twentieth century, the stereotyped roles found in children's literature were so taken for granted that even a discussion of the issue was ignored. Child's (1946), an analysis of children's textbooks, discovered considerable role differentiation between boys and girls in the texts. The study found the girls in the sample to be passive, boys to be active. Girls showed greater affiliation needs; boys attempted to solve problems. Though 20 years old, Child's observations are repeatedly supported by other findings on sex role stereotypes in children's readers (Chase, 1972; Donlan, 1972; Frasher et. al., 1972; Graebner, 1972; Howe, 1971; Jacklin et. al., 1973; Key, 1971, 1972; O'Donnell, 1973; Prida, 1973; Rinsky, 1973; Rose, 1973; Singh 1973 and Tibbets, 1975), in instructional materials (Brody, 1973; Grambs, 1972), in general literature (Cornillion, 1972; Ferguson, 1971; Lieberman, 1972), in social sciences (Acker, 1973; Bart, 1971; Baruch, 1971) and in textbooks in general (Harrison, 1973; Hurst, 1973; Jay and Schnike, 1975; McDowell, 1972; Schmidt, 1971; Wilk, 1973).

In Tennenbaum's *Textbook Town* (1954), boys accomplished goals while girls watched. This image of the male as an active problem-solver, being admired by a passive female spectator, has continued into the seventies. The American Library Association list of Notable Books for Children for 1969 listed two books about boys to every one about girls. Boys in these books are portrayed as independent, competent individuals who do many exciting things while girls are pictured as helpmates performing domestic chores (Whitehurst, 1977:37-38). In another examination of 134 elementary level readers for children, boys dominate in the following traits: cleverness, ingenuity, success in problem solving, strength, bravery, elective helpfulness, acquisition of skills, rewards, adventuresome or imaginative play and altruism. In contrast, the girls dominate in situations highlighting their routine helpfulness, passivity, pseudo-dependence, domesticity, victimization, and humiliation (Women on Words and Images, 1972).

In accord with traditional sex role stereotypes, the textbooks present only male achievers and omit female achievers. Women and girls appear as characters much less frequently than do males. The following ratio of themes is reported in the Women on Words and Images (1972) study: boy-centered stories to girl-centered stories, five to two; adult male main characters to adult female main characters, three to one; male biographies to female biographies, six to one. In their examination of prize-winning books for young children, Weitzman et. al. (1972) report that the females are under-represented by a ratio of 11 to 1 in the illustrations. Counting animals in the illustrations, the ratio increases to 95 male animals to every one female. The Feminists on Children's Literature Study (1971) found that professionally successful female role models with marketplace achievement orientation are rare in American textbooks for children. American history textbooks give little weight to the cultural and social contributions of American women. Male leaders are highlighted even in reform movements in which women participated (Trecker, 1971). Ideas and opinions are attributed to men, not women. In addition to being negligent about the role of the female in history, social studies textbooks also fail to reflect female participation in the labor force and in other aspects of society (Whitehurst, 1977:38; Bragdon and McCutchen, 1967).

Perhaps to legitimize the relegation of women to insignificance, the textbooks also reinforce traditional notions on sexappropriate activities and attitudes. In primary grade texts, fathers go off to various marketplace jobs, and mothers go off to the store to shop. Mother and the children beg dad for money he earns ("Mothers Knit, While Dads Read," Pottker, 1971). In the Women On Words and Images (1972:9) sample of 134 books, one sixth as many occupations are shown for women as for men. While men occupy 147 different jobs, women in the plots occupy only 25 jobs. There are no female doctors, jurists or college professors. The women are shown engaged only in "womanly" occupations: teachers, governesses, dressmakers and telephone operators. In the biographies, 119 plots present the achievements of 88 males, compared to 27 plots which introduce only 17 female subjects.

The vocational choices of children at every age level are reported to reflect the consequences of such sexist occupational socialization. When asked, boys choose occupations which are considered "masculine," girls choose "feminine" occupations (Mussen, Conger, and Kagen, 1963:561-567; Hartley, 1960; Klenmack and Edwards, 1973). In Ahmad's (1974) study of female undergraduates at the University of Delhi, India, only a small number of girls are reported to view marketplace employment as a means of self-fulfillment.

Thus, sexism in textbooks strives to maintain the traditional status quo between the sexes. Just as social inequality is considered "functional" for social stratification, sexism is "functional" in training the male half of the human race for leadership and marketplace achievement while socializing the female half for mainly subservient and support functions.

# Bibliography

ACKER, J. 1973. "Women and Social Stratification: A Case of Intellectual Sexism." *American Journal of Sociology*, 78, 936-945.

ADAMS, D. and FARRELL, P., eds. 1966. Education and Social Development. Syracuse, New York: Center for Development Education, Syracuse University. (Unpublished manuscript).

AHMAD, KARUNA, 1974. "Women's Higher Education: Recruitment and Relevance" in Singh, A. and Altbach, G., eds. 1974 The Higher Learning in India. New Delhi: Vikas.

ALTEKAR, A.S. 1938. The Position of Women in Hindu Civilization. Benares: Culture Publication House, Benares Hindu University Press.

ANONYMOUS. 1971. "Sex Stereotypes in Readers" *Library Journal*, CVI, 680.

ASTHANA, P., 1974. Women's Movement in India. Delhi. Vikas Publishing House.

ATKINSON, J.W. and FEATHER, N.T. eds. 1966. A Theory of Achievement Motivation. New York: Wiley.

BALDWIN, A.L. 1942. "Personality Structure Analysis: A Statistical Method for Investigating Single Personality," *Journal of Abnormal and Social Psychology*, 37, 163-183.

BANDURA, A. and WALTERS, H. 1963. Social Learning and Personality Development. New York: Holt, Rinehart and Winston.

BARBER, B. 1957, Social Stratification. New York: Harcourt, Brace & Co.

BART, P.B. 1971. "Sexism and Social Science," *Journal of Marriage and the Family*, 33, (4), 734-745.

BARUCH, G. 1971. "Research in Psychology Relevant to the Situation of Women," in Modern Language Association of America, New York Commission on the Status of Women, 1971, 197: 26-34.

BASU, A. 1974. The Growth of Education and Political Development in India, 1898-1920. Delhi: Oxford University Press.

BELL, D. 1973. The Coming of Post-Industrial Society. New York: Basic Books.

BERNSTEIN, J. 1972. "The Elementary School: Training Ground for Sex Role Stereotypes," *Personnel and Guidance Journal*, 51, (2), 97-101.

BHASIN, K., ed. 1972, The Position of Women in India: Proceedings of a Seminar Held in Srinagar, September, 1971. Bombay: Leslie Sawhney

Programme of Training for Democracy.

BISWAS, A. and AGGARWAL, J.C. 1972. Education in India, 1971. New Delhi: Arya Book Depot.

BOSS, L. 1974. "Ramifications of Sex Role Stereotypes for the Self-Concepts of Males and Females" (unpublished paper, Purdue University) cited in Deaux, K. 1976. The Behavior of Men and Women. Monterey, California: Brook Cole Publishing Co.

BRAGDON, H.W. and McCUNCHEN, S.P. 1967. History of a Free People. 6th Edition, New York: Macmillan Book Co.

BRODY, C.M. 1973. "Do Instructional Materials Reinforce Sex Stereotyping?" *Educational Leadership*, 31, 119-122.

BROVERMAN, I., *et al.* 1973. "Sex Role Stereotypes: A Current Appraisal" *Mental Health Digest*, 5, 1-6.

BULLOUGH, V.L. 1873, The Subordinate Sex: A History of Attitudes Towards Women. Urbana, Illinois: University of Illinois Press.

CAMPBELL, J. 1962, Masks of God: Oriental Mythology. New York: Viking Press.

CARNEY, T.F. 1972. Content Analysis. Winnipeg: University of Manitoba.

Census of India, 1971, Series 1. 1972, Economic Characteristics of Populations (Selected Tables). Place of publication missing: Registrar General and Census Commissioner, India.

Central Statistical Organization. 1972. Statistical Abstract, India. New Delhi: Department of Statistics, Ministry of Planning, Government of India.

CHAND, K. 1972. Indian Sexology. New Delhi: S. Chand & Co. Pvt. Ltd.

CHASE, D.J. 1972. "Sexism in Textbooks," *Nation's Schools*, XC, 31-35.

CHATTOPADHYAYA, S. 1965. Social Life in Ancient India. Calcutta: Academic Publishers.

Child, I., *et al.* 1946, "Children's Textbooks and Personality Development: An Exploration in the Social Psychology of Education," *Psychological Monographs*, 60, 1-53.

CHOPRA, P.N. 1975. Economic Structure and Activities. The Gazetteer of Indian Union, Vol. III. New Delhi: Ministry of Education and Social Welfare.

CONKLIN G. 1973, "Emerging Conjugal Role Patterns in a Joint Family System: Correlates of Social Change in Dharwar, India." *Journal of Marriage and the Family*, 35, 742-748.

COOMARSWAMY A. 1928, Buddha and the Gospel and Buddhism. London: Harrap.

CORNILLON, S., ed. 1972. Images of Women in Fiction: Feminist Perspectives. Bowling Green, Ohio: Bowling Green University Popular Press.

CURRAN, J.P. 1972. "Differential Effects of Stated Preferences and Questionnaire Role Performance on Interpersonal Attraction in the Dating Situation," *Journal of Psychology*, 82, 313-327.

D'ANDRADE, R.G. 1966. "Sex Differences and Cultural Institutions," in Maccoby, E. and Jacklin, C. 1974 The Psychology of Sex Differences. Standford, California: California University Press.

dE BEAUVOIR S. 1970. The Second Sex (edited and translated by H.M. Parshley), New York: Alfred A. Knopf.

dE RIENCOURT, A. 1974. Sex and Power in History. New York; David McKay.

DAS, H. 1932. Purdah: The Status of Indian Women. London: Kegan Paul, Trench, Trubner.

DECKARD, B. 1975. The Women's Movement: Political, Socio-economic and Psychological Issues. New York: Harper and Row.

DEEGAN D.Y. 1951. The Stereotype of the Single Woman in American Novels: A Social Study with Implications for the Education of Women. New York: King's Crown Press, Columbia University.

DIKSHIT, R. 1964 Women in Sanskrit Dramas. Delhi: Mehar Chand Lachman Das.

Directorate General of Employment and Training (Occupational Information Unit). 1968 (Second Edition) National Classification of Occupations (NCO, 1968), New Delhi: Ministry of Labor, Employment and Rehabilitation, Government of India.

Directorate General of Employment and Training. 1972 Occupational Educational Pattern in India, Private Sector—1967, Part II. New Delhi: Ministry of Labour and Rehabilitation, Government of India.

Directorate General of Employment and Training. 1973 Occupational Pattern in India (Private Sector), Part I, 1969. New Delhi: Ministry of Labor, Government of India.

DONLAN, D. 1972. "The Negative Image of Women in Children's Literature," *Elementary English*, XLIC, 604-611.

BUBOIS J.A. 1928. Hindu Manners, Customs and Ceremonies (Translated by H.K. Beauchamp). Oxford: Oxford University Press.

Education Commission (India). 1965. Recommendations on Women's Education. A Compilation Prepared by the Educatio Commission. New Delhi: Education Commission.

FERGUSON, M. 1971. "The Sexist Image of Women in Literature," in Modern Language Association of American, New York Commission on the Status of Women, 41-48.

FRASHER, R. and WALKAR A. 1972. "Sex Roles in Early Reading Textbooks," *The Reading Teacher*, 25, (8) 741-749.

GAGNON, J.H. and SIMON W. eds. 1973. The Sexual Scence. New Brunswick, New Jersey: Transaction Books.

GEORGE, E.I. and MATHEWS Y.G. 1967. "Ideal Self-Concept in Relation to Sex Roles," *Psychological Studies*, 14, 6-11.

GERSONI-STAVN, D., ed. 1974. Sexism and Youth. New York: R.R. Bowker Company, A Xerox Education Company.

GLAZER-MALBIN, N. WAEHRER H.Y., eds. 1973. Woman in a Man-Made World: A Socioeconomic Handbook. New York: Rand McNally.

GOFFMAN, I 1963. Stigma: Notes on the Management of Spoiled Identity. Englewood Cliffs, New Jersey: Prentice Hall.

GRAEBNER, D.B 1972. "A Decade of Sexism in Readers," *The Reading Teacher*, XXVI, 52-58.

GRAMS, J.D. 1972. "Sex Stereotypes in Instructional Materials, Literature and Language. A Survey of Research." *Women Studies Abstracts,* 1, 91-94.

GRAMS, J.D, and WAETJEN, W.B. 1971, Sex: Does it make a difference? North Scituate, Massachusetts: Duxbury Press.

GUPTA, S.S., ed. 1969. Women in Indian Folklore (Linguistic and Religoius Study): A Short Survey of Their Social Status and Position. Calcutta: Indian Publications, Folklore Series No. 15.

HARRISON, B.G. 1973. Unlearning the Lie: Sexism in School. New York: Liveright.

HARTLEY, R.E. 1960. "Children's Concept of Male and Female Roles," *Merrill Palmer Quarterly,* 6, 83-91.

HOLLINGSWORTH, L.S. 1922. "Differential Actions upon the Sexes of Forces which Tend to Segregate the Feebleminded," in Jenkins, J.J. and Patterson, D.G., eds. 1961 Studies in Individual Differences, New York. Appleton, Century, Crofts.

HOLSTI, O.E. 1969. Content Analysis for Social Sciences and Humanities. Reading, Massachusetts: Addison Wesley.

HOLTER, H. 1972. "Sex Roles ond Social Change" in Saffilios-Rothschild, ed. 1974 Women & Social Policy. Englewood Cliffs, N.J.: Prentice Hall.

HOWE, F. 1971. "Sexual Stereotypes Start Early", Superintendent's Work Conference, July 14, 1971. Also Published in *Saturday Review,* October 15, 1971.

————. 1974. "Sexual Stereotypes and the Public Schools," in Kundsin, R.B. 1974. Women and Success; The Anatomy of Achievement. New York: William Marrow and Co.

HURST, G. 1973. "Sex Bias in Junior High School Literature Anthologies Eric Reprint # ED 085763. St. Louis, Missouri: National Organization for Women, St. Louis Chapter.

India Planning Commission (Education Division). 1968 Report of Steering Committee of Planning Group on Education. New Delhi: Education Division, Planning Commission (mimeographed).

JACKLIN, C.N. and MISCHEL, H.N. 1973. "As the Twig is Bent: Sex Stereotyping in Early Readers," *School of Psychology Digest,* 2, (3), 30-38.

JAY, W.T. and SCHNINKE C.W. 1975. "Sex Bias in Elementary School Mathematics Texts," *The Arithmetic Teacher,* 22, 242-246.

JAYAL, S. 1966. The Status of Women in the Epics. Delhi: Motilal Banarsi Das.

KANUNGO, R. and PANDA, K.C 1966. "Job Perception Among Adolescents," *Indian Journal of Applied Psychology,* 1967, (4), 6.

KAPADIA, K.M. 1966. Marriage and Family in India. Bombay: Oxford University Press.

KENNEDY. B.C. 1973. "On Being A Women—Indian and American: A Comparative Study," Asian Survey, XIII, 833-852.

KEY, M.R. 1971. "A Linguistic Gathers the Evidence: The Role of Male and Female in Children's Books—Dispelling All Doubt," *Wilson Library Bulletin,* 167-176.

KLEMMACK D.L. and EDWARDS, J.N. 1973. ' 'Women's Acquisition of Stereotyped Occupational Aspirations," *Sociology and Social Research*, 57, (4), 510-515.

KUPPUSWAMI, B. 1957. "A Study of Opinion Regarding Marriage and Divorce." Cited in Kapadia, 1966.

LANNOY, R. 1971. The Speaking Tree: A Study of Indian Culture and Society. New York: Oxford University Press.

LIEBERMAN, M.R. 1972. "Some Day My Prince Will Come: Female Acculturation Through the Fairy Tale," *College English*, 34, (3), 383-395.

McDOWELL, M.B. 1972. "Male and Female Chauvinism in the Teaching of Language and Literature." Annual Meeting of the Midwest Modern Language Association, St. Louis, Missouri, October 26-28, 1972. ERIC Reprint # EO77031.

McCLELLAND, D.C., ATKINSON, J.W., CLARK, R.A. and LOWELL, E.G. 1953, The Achievement Motive. New York: Appleton-Century-Crofts.

McCLELLAND, D.C. 1961. The Achieving Society. New York: Van Nostrand Co.

McGRAW HILL Guidelines. 1975. "McGraw Hill Guidelines for Equal Treatment of the Sexes," *School Library Journal*, 21, 23-27.

MAJUMDAR, R.C. 1953. An Advanced History of India, London: Macmillan.

MEDNICK, M.. TANGRI, S. and HOFFMAN, L.W., eds. 1975. Women and Achievement: Social and Motivational Analysis. New York: John Wiley and Sons.

MEYER, J.J. 1953, Sexual Life in Ancient India. New York: Barnes and Noble.

MILLER, C. and SWIFT, K. 1976. Words and Women. New York: Double day.

MILLET, K. 1970. Sexual Politics. New York: Equinox Books.

Ministry of Education and Social Welfare, Government of India. 1974. Education in India. 1968-69. New Delhi: Controller of Publications.

MISRA, R. 1967. Women in Mughal India (1526-1748 A.D.) Delhi: Munshi Ram Manohar Lal.

Modern Language Association of America, New York Commission. On the Status of Women. 1971 Women & Education: A Feminist Perspective (Conference Proceedings November 5-7, 1971). Pittsburgh: Pittsburgh University Press.

MONIER-WILLIAMS, M. 1887. Brahminism and Hinduism. London: J. Murray.

MOORE, W.E. 1965. The Impact of Industry. Englewood Cliffs, New Jersey: Prentice Hall.

————. 1969, "Occupational Socialization" in Goslin, D., ed. 1969. A Handbook of Socialization Theory & Research. Chicago; Rand McNally.

MUKHERJI, I. 1972. Social Status of North Indian Women, 1526-1707 A.D. Agra: Shiv Lal Aggarwala & Co.

MURDOCK, G.P. 1965. Social Structure. New York: Free Press.

NCERT. 1971. Education and National Development: Report of the Education Commission, 1964-66. New Delhi: National Counci lof Educational Research and Training.

———. 1971. Position of Nationalized Textbooks in India. New Delhi: Department of Testbooks, National Institute of Education, NCERT.

National Committee on the Status of Women in India. 1975. A Synopsis of the Report of the National Committee on The Status of Women (1971-1974). New Delhi: Allied Publishers.

O'DONNELL, R.W. 1973. "Sex Bias in Primary Social Studies Textbooks," *Educational Leadership*, 31, (2), 137-141.

OAKLEY, A. 1976. Women's Work: The Housewife, Past and Present. New York: Vintage Books.

POOL, I.D., ed. 1959. Trends in Content Analysis. Urbana: University of Illinois Press.

POTTKER, J.M. 1971. "Female Stereotypes in Elementary School Textbooks," Cited in Grams and Waetjen, 1975.

PRATT, A.V. 1976. "The New Feminist Criticism: Exploring the History of the New Space" in Roberts. I., ed. 1976.

PRIDA, D., *et al.* (Compilers) 1973 "The Portrayal of Women in Children's Books on Puerto Rican Themes," in Feminists Look at the 100 Books. New York: Council on Interracial Books for Children.

PYUN, C.S. 1973. "The Monetary Value of a Housewife," in Glazer-Malbin *et al.*, eds., 1973.

RAGHUVANSHI, V.P.S. 1969. Indian Society in the Eighteenth Century. New Delhi: Associated Publishing House.

RAWAT, P.L. 1970. History of Indian Education. Agra. Ram Prasad & Sons.

The Research and Reference Division, Ministry of Information and Broadcasting, Government of India, Compiler. 1975 India: A Reference Manual, 1975. New Delhi: Publications Division, Ministry of Information and Broadcasting, Government of India.

———. 1976. India: A Reference Manual, 1976. New Delhi: Publications Division, Ministry of Information and Broadcasting, Government of India.

RINSKY, L.A. 1973. "Equality of the Sexes and Children's Literature," *Elementary English*, 50; (7), 1075-1092.

RITZER, G. 1972. Man and His Work: Conflict and Change. New York: Appleton-Century-Crofts.

ROBERTS, J.I., ed. 1976. Beyond Intellectual Sexism: A New Women, A New Reality. New York: David McKay.

ROSE, K. 1973. "Sleeping Beauty Awakes: Children's Literature and Sex Role Myths." Annual Meeting of the National Council of Teachers of English, Philadelphia, November 22-24, 1973. ERIC Reprint SED089322.

ROSS, A.D. 1961. The Hindu Family in its Urban Setting. Toronto: Toronto University Press.

ROSSI, A.S. 1965. "Equality Between the Sexes: An Immodest Proposal" in Lifton, R.J., ed. 1965. The Women in America. Cambridge

Massachusetts: Houghton Mifflin.

————. 1969. "Sex Equality, the Beginning of Ideology," in Roszak, B. and Roszak T., eds. 1969. New York; Harper & Row.

SCHMIDT, D.B. 1971. "Sexism in Textbooks" in Modern Language Association of America, 82-87. New York Commission on the Status of Women.

SCHNAILBERG, A. 1970. "Measuring Modernism: Theoretical and Empirical Explorations," *American Journal of Sociology*, 76, 399-425.

Scott, Foresman & Co. 1972. Guidelines for Improving the Image of Women in Textbooks. Glenview, Illinois: Scott, Foresman & Co. ERIC Reprint # ED076957.

SEARS, R.R., MACCOBY, E.E. and LEVINE, H. 1957. Patterns of Child Rearing. Evanston, Illinois: Row, Peterson and Company.

SEKHAR, A.C. 1974. "1971 Census—A Statistical Outline," in Bose, A. et. al., eds. 1974. Population in India's Development: 1947-2000. Delhi: Vikas Publishing House.

SEWARD, G.H. and WILLIAMSON, R.C., eds. 1970· Sex Roles in Changing Society. New York: Random House.

SHARMA, B. 1966. Social Life in Northern India (600-1000 A.D.). Delhi: Munshiram Manoharlal.

SHRIDHARANI, KRISHANLAL. 1941. My India, My America. New York: Duell, Sloan & Pearce, Inc.

SINGH, J.M. 1973. "Language, Education and Ethnic Children's Literature at Penn State University," Annual Meeting of the National Council of Teachers of English, Philadelphia, November 22-24, 1973.

SINHA, A.K.P. and DASH, J.K. 1959. "A Study of Occupational Choices of College Students," *Indian Journal of Psychology*, 34, (3), 135-141.

SINHA, S.N. 1970. "Men and Women of India Today" in Seward and Williamson, eds. 1970.

STAVN, D.G. 1972. "Reducing the 'Miss Muffet Syndrome': An Annotated Bibliography," *School Library Journal*, 66-70.

STEIN, A.M. and BAILEY M.M. 1975. "The Socializatio of Achievement Motivation in Females," in Mednick, Tangri and Hoffman, 1975.

STOLL, C.S. 1974. Female and Male: Socialization, Social Roles, and Social Structure. Dubuque, Iowa: Wm. C. Brown Company Publishers.

STONE, P.J., DUNPHY, D.C., Smith, M.S., OGLIVIE, D.M. and Associates. 1966. The General Enquirer: A Computer Approach to Content Analysis. Cambridge, Massachusetts: M.I.T. Press.

The Feminists on Children's Literature. 1971. "A Feminist Looks at Children's Literature," *School Library Journal*, 17, (5), 19-29,

THIRTHA, N.V. and THIRTHA, L. 1972. Education and Social Change, Bangalore: Center for Educational Sociology, Department of Post-graduate Studies in Education, Bangalore University.

THOMAS, P. 1964. Indian Women Through the Ages: A Historical Survey of the Position of Women and the Institutions of Marriage and Family in India from Remote Antiquity to the Present Day. Bombay: Asia Publishing House.

TIBBETS, S.L   1975. "Children's Literature—A Feminist Viewpoint.," *California Journal of Educational Research*, 26, 1-5.

TITTLE, C.K. *et al.* 1974. Women and Educational Testing: A Selective Review of the Research Literature and Testing Practices. Princeton, New Jersey: Educational Testing Service.

TRECKER, J.L. 1971. "Women's Place in the Curriculum," *Saturday Review*, October 15, 1971, 88-92.

TREIMAN, D.J. 1976. "Problems of Concept and Measurement in the Comparative Study of Occupational Mobility," *Social Science Research*, 4, 183-240.

UPADHYAYA, B.S. 1974. Women in Rgveda. Delhi: S. Chand & Co.

VYAS, S.N. 1967. Indian in the Ramayana Age: A Study of the Social and Cultural Conditions in Ancient India as Described in Valmiki's Ramayana. Delhi: Atma Ram & Sons.

WEBER, M. 1946. "The Social Psychology of the World Religions," in H.H. Gerth and C.W. Mills, eds., 1946 from Max Weber: Essays in Sociology. New York: Oxford University Press.

WEITZMAN, L.J., Effier, D., Holoda, E. and Ross, C. 1972, "Sex-role Socialization in Picture Books for Pre-school Children," *American Jonrnal of Sociology*, 77, 1125-1150.

WHITEHURST, C.D. 1977. Women in America: The Oppressed Majority. Santa Monica, California: Goodyear Publishing Co.

WIIK, L. 1973. "The Sexual Bias of the Textbook Literature," *English Journal*, 62 (2), 224-229.

Women on Words and Images. 1972. Dick and Jane as Victims: Sex stereotyping in Children's Readers. Princeton, New Jersey: Women on Words and Images.

ZIMET, S.G., ed., 1972. What Children Read in School: Critical Analysis of Primary Reading Textbooks. New York: Grune & Stratton, Inc.

# Index